BOOKCELLAR
FREEBIE

Beyond the Myth of Marital Happiness

Beyond the Myth of Marital Happiness

How Embracing the Virtues of Loyalty, Generosity, Justice, and Courage Can Strengthen Your Relationship

Blaine J. Fowers, Ph.D.

JOSSEY-BASS
A Wiley Company
San Francisco

Jossey-Bass books and products are available through most bookstores. To contact Jossey-Bass directly, call (888) 378-2537, fax to (800) 605-2665, or visit our website at www.josseybass.com.

Substantial discounts on bulk quantities of Jossey-Bass books are available to corporations, professional associations, and other organizations. For details and discount information, contact the special sales department at Jossey-Bass.

 Manufactured in the United States of America on Lyons Falls Turin Book. This paper is acid-free and 100 percent totally chlorine-free.

Library of Congress Cataloging-in-Publication Data

Fowers, Blaine J., date.
  Beyond the myth of marital happiness : how embracing the virtues of loyalty, generosity, justice, and courage can strengthen your relationship / by Blaine J. Fowers.
     p.   cm.
  ISBN 0-7879-4567-6
1. Marriage.   2. Marriage—Psychological aspects.   I. Title.
  HQ734 .F722 2000
  306.81—dc21

                                                            00-008753

FIRST EDITION
HB Printing   10 9 8 7 6 5 4 3 2 1

⟨ Contents

Beyond the Myth of
Marital Happiness

To Susan
for the happiness we share
and for the beauty of your generosity and loyalty
that make our partnership possible

Part I

The Myth

1

The Guidance of Myth

*We suffer primarily not from our vices or our weak-
nesses, but from our illusions. We are haunted, not
by reality, but by those images we have put in place of
reality.*

　　　　　　　　　　Daniel J. Boorstin, The Image[1]

One of our most cherished desires today is to have a satisfying
marriage. Our popular culture is saturated with images of romantic fulfillment and formulas for achieving a happy marriage. So
why do so many of us begin marriages with such high hopes, only
to see those dreams end in divorce? A persistent and unprecedented
level of divorce makes our deeply held aspirations for marriage
harder and harder to maintain. **This is the paradox of marriage: our
deep desire for a happy marriage leads to the strange situation in
which marriage is both more valued and more fragile than ever
before.**

When you sit back and think about it, doesn't it amaze you that
we simply accept the discouraging brittleness of marriage as normal
and somehow inevitable? We struggle with this paradox, we worry
about our own and our loved ones' chances for a lifelong, fulfilling
marriage, and we fret about the fragile state of marriage. But we end
up feeling resigned to this situation, partly because it is just so difficult to identify a real alternative.

In the beginning of my career as a marital researcher and therapist, I was just as captivated by the ideal of marital happiness as anyone else. My research focused on understanding what makes marriages satisfying. As I have studied marriage and reflected on my own and others' marriages, however, I have come to question the stunning consensus we see among marital researchers, therapists, the media, and the public about how to make marriage work. Just about anyone will tell you that marriages are good when they are satisfying and that communication is the key to making a marriage satisfying. If we all know how to make a marriage satisfying and we all desperately want good marriages, why do we have so much trouble bringing it off?

Our predicament with marriage is due to a historic misunderstanding of marriage. The evolution of marriage in our civilization has led us to expect marriage to make us happy and provide us with an emotionally fulfilling life. Those high expectations make it all too easy for us to become disillusioned, and divorce is a natural response to our disappointment. Consequently, contemporary marriage contains a volatile mixture of importance and fragility, hope and despair, allure and disappointment.

I wrote this book to offer an explanation of the paradox of marriage and to present a fresh approach to marriage that will help us renew and enrich our relationships. I want to share my conviction with you that the best marriages are partnerships in which spouses are devoted to creating a shared life that is larger than the emotional payoff of the marriage. A couple creates a strong marriage by embracing a set of ideals and goals toward which the partners strive together. When marriage becomes a partnership devoted to worthwhile aims, it gives us more than emotional satisfaction; it helps to make our lives rich and meaningful. Couples in partnership marriages do experience happiness in their relationships, but there is much more to their marriages than emotional attachment. The teamwork that brings a couple's dreams to life and allows the partners to enjoy their accomplishments together adds a crucial dimension to a partnership marriage.

Couples have many different goals, from ordinary aims (such as bringing children up well) to the pursuit of public service or the cultivation of special talents or abilities. Some couples can tell you what their aims are; others simply live their ideals without spelling them out. We will see how the virtues of partnership—friendship, loyalty, generosity, self-restraint, and justice—can help us have vibrant, lasting marriages and provide a profound sense of belonging and meaning in our lives. Some readers will find that this book simply shows them how better to appreciate and foster the goodness that already exists in their marriages. For others, this book will open up new possibilities to develop a flourishing marriage.

The Myth of Marital Happiness

The paradox of marriage has led me to see the ideal of marital happiness as a guiding myth in American life. I do not mean that aspiring to marital bliss is simply mistaken or wrong; many people are happily married, and this kind of shared happiness is a wonderful thing. I think it is important for you to know that I treasure the happiness that I experience with my wife, Susan. I did not write this book because I have been disappointed with marriage. Instead, my life with Susan has taught me that there is so much more to a good marriage than happiness and satisfaction. I decided to write this book when I recognized that so few writers on marriage discuss the richer aspects of marriage. Marital happiness creates one kind of attachment between partners, but we will find that there are other kinds of ties between partners that are stronger and richer.

I am calling our collective expectations for a happy marriage a *myth* because this aspiration is larger than life and has come to be the only widely accepted basis for marriage in our society. *The majority* of marriages fall far short of that ideal: about half of all couples divorce, and many others remain married in spite of their dissatisfaction.[2] In addition, experiencing marriage as satisfying virtually requires us to have *positive illusions* about our relationships. We adopt these illusions to help us fulfill our excessive expectations for marital happiness. Our pursuit of an almost unreachable goal makes the seeking of marital happiness a kind of mythic quest.

Myths and Everyday Life

In a fascinating series of books, lectures, and interviews, Joseph Campbell teaches us that myths are not simply ancient falsehoods that were required by immature peoples of the past. He shows us that myths are necessary for a meaningful communal life, including our own. **I am using the term myth in the sense that Campbell prefers: to recognize that certain stories or metaphors remind us of important truths about how to cope with the harsh, often unendurable realities of life.** In one of his luminous interviews with Bill Moyers, Campbell says, "The myth tells me about [life], how to respond to certain crises of disappointment or delight or failure or success. The myth tells me where I am."[3] These larger-than-life stories are important because they help us recognize our place in the world. A society's myths express its common understanding of what life is about. Without these kinds of shared ideas about living, we would feel quite lost and alone. Myths present a set of ideals to us, along with models of behavior and outlook. In this way, mythological stories are an essential kind of guidance for how to live.

We moderns tend to think that we are beyond the need for myths. After all, don't we live in a time enlightened by a science that teaches us the realities of our existence in time and space? A central theme of our modern story is the belief that we have been liberated from the darkness and ignorance of myth and tradition and have thereby progressed into the light of true understanding. We believe that modern progress requires us to let go of old myths about the world and human life because we have discovered that these myths don't match the facts—they are not literally true. And yet we do rely on myths, just as Campbell suggests. For example, in their wonderful book *Habits of the Heart*,[4] Robert Bellah and his colleagues remind us that the cowboy and the intrepid private detective (à la Sam Spade) are important mythic heroes for us because of their strength, virtue, and incorruptibility.

Beginnings of the Ideal of Marital Happiness

In the same way, our larger-than-life ideal of marriage may be best understood as a myth that has been reinforced by an even older tradition of storytellers. Campbell cites the twelfth-century troubadours as one of the sources of our understanding of love and marriage. Their songs and tales helped formulate a new ideal of courtly love, a form of romantic love that was strictly separated from and incompatible with marriage.

This incompatibility is expressed in the epic poem of Tristan and Isolde, historically one of the most important and influential love stories of our civilization.[5] In this tale, Tristan is wounded in battle, and no one in his home country of Cornwall can heal him. He sets out in a ship to search for a healer, and the wind blows him to Ireland. He is brought to Isolde, who nurses him back to health.

After Tristan returns home, he is sent out in search of a wife for his uncle, King Mark. Tristan and his companions are fatefully blown back to Ireland. When they reach the shore, they find that a dragon has so distressed the kingdom that the king of Ireland is offering the hand of his daughter, Isolde, to whoever will slay the beast. Tristan kills the dragon and is given Isolde, but he announces that instead of marrying her, he will take her to Cornwall to become King Mark's wife because that was his quest.

Isolde's mother prepares a potion for King Mark and Isolde to drink so that they will love each other, and a nurse is given charge of the potion. But on the voyage back to Cornwall, she mistakenly gives it to Tristan and Isolde. They are seized with love for each other and consummate their passion immediately.

This creates a tremendous problem, of course, as Tristan is now in love with his uncle's (the king's) fiancée. When the nurse realizes what has happened, she tells Tristan that he has drunk his death. Tristan replies, "If by my death, you mean this agony of love, that is my life. If by my death, you mean the punishment that we are to suffer if discovered, I accept that. And if by my death, you mean eternal punishment in the fires of hell, I accept that, too."[6]

For the sake of his love, Tristan is willing to relinquish his position in the world, his life, and even his eternal salvation. The remainder of the poem tells how the lovers steal moments together, are discovered by the king's nobles, narrowly escape the punishment of death, and endure many years of hardship in the forest to live out their love. It is a *very* romantic story because Tristan and Isolde are willing to suffer so much for their love.

In this story we have many of the elements of our modern view of love, with two important exceptions. The first is that most of us would not recognize the obligation that Tristan had to bring Isolde to King Mark. The storytellers, even though they recognize the legitimacy of Tristan's obligation to Mark, side unabashedly with the lovers. The second difference is that, for the poets, this story is about the *opposition* of romantic love and marriage, whereas in our recent history we have attempted to *combine* romantic love and marriage in a way that people in the twelfth century would have thought extremely unwise. We moderns, with very different eyes, read the story as a cautionary tale about the consequences of *failing* to unite love and marriage.

Modern Love Stories

In spite of these differences, the tale of Tristan and Isolde prefigures much in our modern view of marriage. The magic of love is symbolized in the potion, but today we also see love as magical. We see love's magic as a powerful, spontaneous experience that comes upon us, often without warning and usually beyond our will. Tristan is brought to Isolde by the winds of fate, just as for us, too, love often has a powerful sense of inevitability for us, too.

For example, Kevin, an interviewee in one of the studies my colleagues and I conducted, described in very magical terms his first encounter with his future fiancée, Helene. They met at a daycare center when he dropped off his son. It was a chance meeting, but their initial attraction was very strong. "She looked at me, and I looked at her, and we stood like that for two minutes, and that was it. It was really spontaneous." They did not date at the time, because

Helene was married. Even when they did begin to spend time with each other, it was rocky at first. Kevin was not sure he wanted to develop a relationship with Helene. But once he allowed himself to become involved, "it just came together—*it was like a miracle.*"

In a separate interview, Helene told the story of their initial meeting in a very similar way: "There was a *chemistry* between us right from the beginning. When we saw each other, it was like love at first sight, and we weren't in a position to talk to each other or go out with each other, and we didn't for quite a while after we met. I was married to someone else. And then we started dating, and we just have a very intense relationship, we have a very strong connection to each other, and I guess it just felt natural. It felt so natural all along." The contemporary references to "chemistry" and "a miracle" are no accident. They clearly express an experience quite similar to the workings of a love potion.

Countless stories, from the tale of Romeo and Juliet to the enormous variety of romance novels and romantic movies, tell us that the experience of love is worth the risk of death, dishonor, impoverishment, and misery. The archetype of Tristan and Isolde is retold again and again, with the barrier between the lovers recast as political or clan-related disputes, as religious, ethnic, or class differences, or as difficulties created by social conventions. And, just like the twelfth-century poets, we always side with the lovers and against the barriers to their love. Indeed, these stories are a way of repeatedly reaffirming that romantic love can and should overcome all obstacles.

This is just the way a myth works. It tells us what is important, what is worth struggling to attain in spite of obstacles. Myths are contained in the stories that we tell about what is crucial to living the best kind of life. In our time, the preeminent form of storytelling is film. There are countless portrayals of loving, satisfying relationships in the movies. In most of these stories, the couple has to overcome substantial barriers to love, and the resolution or culmination of the story is usually the triumph of love. The storyteller, by ending the story with the promise of harmonious love, shows us what it means to live well. We see this both in tales of life-changing love and in stories about the misery and emptiness that plague those who forgo love.

The dominant story of marriage in our culture is the story of falling in love and finding fulfillment in a love relationship. We seldom question this culturally dictated story of marriage or the idea that the *feeling* of love is the engine that makes marriages go. The idea that love is primarily or only a feeling is an important part of the myth of marital happiness. Real love is not a feeling like sadness or anger, which is transitory and focused on particular situations. If we believe that love is only a feeling, we tend to confuse it with *attraction to* or *infatuation with* someone. The experiences of attraction and infatuation are often an important part of love, particularly at the beginning, but they fall far short of capturing the depth and breadth of real love. In real life, love is much more than a feeling. It is a long series of decisions to be together and give to one another, a commitment to work together to build a shared life, a day-to-day involvement that changes who we are as people. Love involves your entire being; your love for someone is a part of you because it involves your feelings, your thoughts, and your actions.

As we will see, there is more than one way to tell the story of marriage. This recognition can liberate us from believing that there is just one way to have a good marriage.

Consequences of the Myth

What I am suggesting in this book is that the dominant story of marriage places too much emphasis on the emotional aspects of marriage, particularly on whether the marriage is satisfying. But how can we know whether our ideals for a happy marriage are excessive?

One indicator is relatively obvious: if we as a culture are expecting too much of marriage, then we are likely to see a great many marriages failing to live up to these expectations. And the evidence is unmistakable: there are about a million divorces in the United States every year. Another way to see that we are expecting too much is that couples have positive illusions about their marriages—that is, in order to maintain their marital happiness, people must see their spouses and their marriages in an unrealistically positive light.

Marital Expectations and Divorce

The recent acceleration of the divorce rate in the United States is nothing short of stunning. There was a gradual increase in the divorce rate between colonial times and the middle of the twentieth century, but a particularly spectacular increase came between 1960 and 1980. During that time the divorce rate more than doubled, and it has stayed relatively stable since the middle of the 1980s. The increase is even more striking when we take a longer-term perspective: in 1880, about 7 percent of marriages ended in divorce, whereas current estimates of the percentage of couples who will divorce vary from 42 percent to 60 percent.[7] Isn't it startling that marriages are between six and nine times more likely to be dissolved now than in 1880? As we will see in Chapter Three, this spectacular rise in the divorce rate has kept pace with the expansion of our expectations for marriage over the last several centuries. These marital ideals are extremely attractive, but we must ask ourselves whether we are paying too high a price for them.

Americans' attitudes about divorce have shifted dramatically during the last one hundred years. At the beginning of the twentieth century, most people saw the increasing frequency of divorce as a catastrophe; in the 1960s, however, attitudes began to shift dramatically toward the acceptance of divorce as a part of life. Divorce was no longer a problem. In fact, it came to be seen as an individual's right.

In recent years, many people have begun to reconsider the negative effects of divorce. We have heard about the distress it brings to almost all children of divorce in the short term, and about the negative effects that some children suffer throughout their lives. Divorcing adults also experience depression and anxiety. Moreover, the risk of suicide doubles after a divorce. For these reasons, some people have identified divorce as the central problem in American families. One of the popular solutions for the high divorce rate is to make a divorce more difficult to obtain.

I think we are right to worry about what the high rate of divorce means about marriage, but divorce is not the problem. It is a symptom of the real problem, which is that we simply expect too many emotional benefits from marriage. As long as we have these excessive expectations, the divorce rate will remain high. Making divorce harder to obtain will only force unhappy spouses to seek creative ways of getting around the law, just as they did before divorce law became more permissive.

Divorce is not always simply the result of excessive expectations, of course, or of permissive divorce laws. For example, many spouses experience intractable misery as a result of ongoing abuse, addiction, and infidelity, which can make marriage unendurable. Such a marriage does not even meet minimal standards for a decent life, and divorce is the only reasonable option. Nevertheless, most divorces are more a result of disappointment than of abuse, addiction, or infidelity.

Excessive Expectations and Illusions

The second way we can see that our marital expectations are too high is that almost all of us distort our perceptions of our marriages to make our relationships seem closer to our ideals. Spouses who are happily married almost invariably see their partners and their marriages in unrealistically positive ways. *In other words, the myth of marital happiness makes it necessary for spouses to harbor positive illusions in order to feel satisfied about their marriages.*

These illusions show up among spouses in several ways. In studies spanning sixty years, over 80 percent of spouses told researchers that they had above-average marriages; fewer than 10 percent said that they had below-average marriages. People who were happy with their marriages gave their partners more credit than they gave themselves for the good things in the marriage, blaming themselves for problems more than they blamed their partners.[8]

One of the clearest indicators that positive illusions are at work is the way in which spouses estimate their own chances of divorce. What would you say if I asked you to tell me how likely it is that your marriage will end in divorce? Go ahead. Think about it. I have been asking people this question for some years now in my research, and I have found their answers extremely interesting. On average, people tell me that their chance of experiencing a divorce in their current marriage is 10 percent or less, but the most common answer that people give to this question is that there is *no chance* that they will divorce! Almost all the people who tell me this know perfectly well that the probability of divorce is much higher for people in general, but they are sure that they are different from other people. In fact, almost all of us believe that we have a lower chance of divorce than other people do. Very, very few people tell me that their chances of divorce are anywhere near the 40 to 60 percent likelihood for couples in general.

Because almost all of us believe that we are very unlikely to divorce, we are seeing the future of our marriages in an unrealistically positive way. For this reason, I call this belief a positive illusion about marriage. For some people, of course, the probability of experiencing a divorce is lower than average. Many factors decrease a couple's likelihood of divorce: being very happily married, having excellent communication, being extremely committed to the marriage, or simply being married for a long time. But I do not believe that people are basing their predictions about their chances of divorce on some statistically driven calculation of realistic odds; rather, they are expressing their fond hopes about the lifelong duration of their marriages.

My favorite anecdote about underestimating the likelihood of divorce involves the research group of students and colleagues with whom I have been working on these studies for the past few years. One day I decided to ask them about their own chances of divorce.

These are people who are very knowledgeable about marriage, divorce, and positive illusions. Guess what they said? They were just as optimistic about the future of their own marriages as our research participants were. (And just in case you're wondering, I think my own chances of divorce are much less than 50 percent, too.) Clearly, at least some of us are deluding ourselves, but all of us fervently hope that our low estimates of our own likelihood of divorce will prove accurate!

Positive illusions about marriage are an outgrowth of the myth of marital happiness, just as divorce is. It makes no sense to try to talk people out of their positive illusions, which are necessary in order for spouses to be satisfied with their marriages. In a study of mine involving more than five thousand couples, every single individual who was happy with his or her marriage was also unrealistic about it. These positive illusions are the best demonstration of the myth: the only people happy with their marriages are those who see their relationships in an unrealistically positive way.

Aside from any discomfort we might have with self-deception, positive illusions are problematic because they tend to be extreme and are a double-edged sword, as I have seen in two of my professional roles. Almost all the couples I encounter as a marital researcher are happily married and are engaged in maintaining positive illusions. Virtually all the couples I have seen as a marital therapist have distorted their perceptions of one another and their marriages in a negative direction; they have accentuated the negative. I now realize that these apparent opposites are two sides of the same coin: either spouses see their marriages in unrealistically positive ways or they interpret everything that happens in the most negative terms.

Metaphorically speaking, this situation is very much like a balance-testing apparatus I have seen. Imagine a board about eighteen inches square that is placed on the apex of a triangular base; the base rests on the floor. To test your balance, you stand on the balancing board with one foot on each side of the board without letting the board touch the floor on either side. This is very difficult, and no one manages it for more than a few seconds.

A balanced view of your marriage is just as difficult to maintain; we tend to lean one way or the other. In this metaphor, the triangular base is our emphasis on happiness in marriage. The natural result of our high expectations about marriage is unsteadiness: we see our relationships either too positively or too negatively. The myth of marital happiness has created this perverse pair of extremes, which leave spouses with the stark choice between seeing their marriages as too good to be true or as no good at all. This is a serious problem. When positive illusions begin to slip, spouses can move very quickly into seeing each other in the worst possible light. In later chapters we will see how adding other supports to the balancing board, such as shared goals and virtues, can help stabilize this balance of positive and negative perceptions of the marriage.

Beyond the Paradox of Marriage

Myths help to define a culture, and people take the truth and power of myths for granted. It is very difficult to question the myths by which we live. They seem obviously true to those of us who share them, and questioning them seems to verge on nonsense (some readers, no doubt, will also see my view of marriage as verging on nonsense for just that reason). The myth of marital happiness is so familiar to us that it is difficult for us to really see it or recognize it as a set of problematic historical ideas. One of the hallmarks of a functioning myth is that people see it as the truth rather than as one of many possible interpretations of life. Questioning a prevailing myth is also emotionally difficult. We are tremendously attached to these stories, and we want very much to live them out ourselves.

Yet the unfortunate consequences of the myth of marital happiness make it clear that a shift is necessary in our cultural understanding of marriage. Does this mean that we should give up on love, satisfaction, intimacy, emotional support, good communication, and good sex in marriage? No. Does it mean that marriage must be grimly continued on the sole basis of commitment? No. Am I suggesting that no one should divorce? No. Is any of these propositions even a possibility for us? No. I believe that it is neither possible nor desirable to simply discard our cultural ideals. Anyway, even if we thought it was a good idea, we could not abandon these kinds of deeply felt values all at once.

Instead of revolutionizing marriage, I suggest that we begin to reinterpret it by broadening and deepening our thinking about what a good marriage is. In our understanding of a good marriage, we can make room for happiness but also for far richer and more enduring aspects of our shared lives.

What We Have Forgotten About Marriage

One of the best places to look for an alternative perspective on marriage is to pay attention to what the popular ideal leaves out. As I contemplated writing this book, I reviewed many of the hundreds of professional and popular books and articles on marriage. I was struck by their nearly exclusive emphasis on the personal benefits of marriage and communication, and by their neglect of other vital aspects of a good marriage. It *is* good to be able to communicate clearly and effectively, to be happy together, and to have a good sexual relationship. There is no doubt that improvements in these areas can make some marriages better. But are good feelings and good communication really the most important aspects of marriage? These books do not even come close to describing the depth and meaning that I have experienced in my own marriage or that I have observed in the strong marriages I see all around me. The popular and professional literature seems to miss the real sources of strength in marriage: the shared goals, the necessary struggles and sacrifices, the calm joy of teamwork, and the comfort in two people carrying out mundane tasks together. All these elements forge the profound bonds that characterize a strong marriage.

One Couple's Story

To illustrate, let me describe how one couple, Annette and Greg, worked through their unrealistic and ultimately discouraging romantic ideals and won through to an enriched view of marriage. In many ways, they are typical. What is unusual about them as a couple is their success in getting beyond the myth of marital happiness. Their story illustrates how marriage can become a partnership that provides belonging, meaning, and purpose through the pursuit of shared goals.

When they met, in college, Annette and Greg were convinced that they were about to embark on a wonderful romantic adventure. They fell in love soon after they started dating, and they were sure that they would always feel as engrossed in and passionate about each other as they did then. Annette says, "I thought it would be like a romantic novel or movie. I would fall in love, and my life would be filled with that love and always stay that way. Nothing would change it; no fights or problems would jar our happiness." Greg felt very attracted to Annette, and he thought that the fascination and excitement would never end. Both Annette and Greg knew that there would be some difficulties; after all, neither of their parents' marriages was even close to their dream. But somehow their love was going to be different.

After a nine-month courtship, they married. Very soon afterward, Annette and Greg began to experience serious discrepancies between their romantic hopes and the realities of married life. They had fallen in love, and they thought that nothing would change their passion and happiness—no arguments, household chores, or demands from the outside world would intrude on their love.

All these normal experiences did become a part of their life together, of course. Annette, in hindsight, believes that she was very naive to have expected anything else. The first few years of marriage seemed to tear at her fond hopes. There was a great deal to be happy

about, but she also found that much of her dream was simply unavailable in her actual marriage. She had to come to terms with the
difference between fantasy and actuality, and whenever she dwelled
on that difference, she would become discouraged and feel like giving up. She thought about divorce, but it never seemed to be a real
option, even after a nasty fight or during a particularly tense period.

In the second year of her marriage to Greg, Annette gave birth
to a son. She and Greg were overjoyed to have a child, but becoming parents changed the way they thought about their marriage.
Greg describes these early years as a period in which he was con-
sumed by concerns about completing college and being able to earn
enough money to support his wife and child. The passionate aspects
of their marriage receded somewhat, given the importance of these
worries for Greg, as well as the energy and love they both devoted
to the nurturing of their young son.

Over the course of eight or ten years, Annette learned to recognize that the reality of her marriage was not so bad. It did not
measure up to her original expectations, but she recognized that few
of the realities of life fulfill one's dreams entirely. She came to see
that her disappointment was due to her having expected too much.
As she learned to focus her attention on what she and Greg actually shared, she found that they had a strong, positive partnership.

Today she says, "Greg is doing well, our two children are doing
well, we have worked together to educate ourselves, and we both
have good occupations and incomes. As I realized what was good
about Greg, rather than paying so much attention to what irritated
me, it was much easier to be content with that. He has so many
abilities that I couldn't dream of even attempting, and he adores
me. He loves me like no one else ever has, even after I have hurt or
disappointed him."

Although it may sound as if Annette has simply shifted to a
slightly more mature but still basically romantic vision of marriage,
the word *love* means much more to her than a romantic feeling. In
the early years of the relationship, love meant emotional excite-

ment, kissing, sex, and romance. Those experiences remain important to Annette, but they have become less prominent. She finds her concept of love difficult to describe: "It is not so much a need for him, but he has become a part of me—what I am is part him, and what he is, is part me. I think a lot less about what I get out of the relationship and more about what I can give to it. I think a lot about how I can keep our togetherness going and about how it is good for our children. We are a couple in love, and we have lived through a lot of difficult times. We work through those problems together and always come back to that love. I've seen it grow stronger and deeper as a result."

Working out their difficulties did not come easily to Annette and Greg. Annette tended to shy away from conflict, whereas Greg liked to dive right in and reach the quickest possible resolution. They experienced very trying conflicts over their relationships with Greg's mother, over finances, and over household responsibilities. Greg's romantic vision was shaken by these conflicts, which emerged in the first months of their marriage. He was completely astonished by Annette's ability to turn away from him in anger and leave him feeling dismissed and entirely disarmed. This was all the more disconcerting because Greg had always had a pugnacious bent that allowed him to hold his own in any kind of fight.

The key backdrop to their ability to resolve their difficulties is *they were always able to see that their marriage was more important than the problems they were facing*. Annette emphasizes that it "took a strong feeling that we wanted to stay together so we could work out our pain and disagreements." Her ability to maintain this commitment in the face of their difficulties is something she attributes to a family history that has included almost no divorce in previous generations, and to a religious upbringing that strongly encouraged lasting marital commitment. That heritage is extremely helpful. In the end, however, it is not enough by itself.

Annette and Greg had to carry their commitment through their own struggles and uncertainties. Annette believes that her love for

Greg, in addition to her respect for herself and for the promise she made by marrying him, gave her the strength to stick out the difficult times. "It sounds so healthy and natural," she says, "but it is not that easy when you are going through it." Greg expresses a similar bedrock loyalty to the marriage that superseded the disgruntled feelings he experienced at times.

Greg also describes a new kind of respect and love that emerged over time in their marriage. He began to see Annette as more than a wife—as someone with a great reservoir of untapped talents and abilities. He became devoted to encouraging her to develop her potential by taking college courses and, eventually, becoming a professional.

Annette often questioned whether she could achieve her goals, but their teamwork provided indispensable support for her efforts. By the time she returned to college, they had two children. Greg took more time to watch them, took a second job, and encouraged her success at every turn. He saw Annette's goals and his own subsequent higher education as joint projects on which they embarked as a couple.

"The projects were more than just projects," he says. "They were always something that was good for the family. There are many projects that I wanted to be involved in, but most of them fell by the wayside because they were not good for the family."

Annette and Greg did not see their educational or career pursuits as expressions of personal ambition that they were imposing on the family. Their choices of shared projects were always guided by what was best for their family: financial well-being, an environment in which their children could develop friendships with other good kids, and their own ability to play a constructive part in their community.

Renewing Marriage

Greg's and Annette's story illustrates the four themes I want to share with you in this book about how to enrich your marriage:

1. Shifting the focus from emotional gratification to partnership in marriage

2. Developing a shared vision of the kind of marriage you want to have

3. Practicing virtue in marriage

4. Understanding how marriage helps us create meaningful ties to many people

The beauty of what I will recommend is that it is already accessible to us. In fact, many couples already do much of what I will suggest. The difficulty is that these enriching alternatives are, in a way, hidden from us because they are not part of our normal way of thinking about marriage. We will explore the unnoticed strengths that are present in most marriages, and I will provide a vocabulary that will help you appreciate and expand on the goodness that is already in your marriage.

From Emotional Gratification to Partnership

If our feelings about our marriages do not provide a good foundation for strong and lasting relationships, what will? I have become convinced that the strength and the happiness of good marriages are both rooted in the partners' mutual commitment to the creation of a shared life. The best marriages are characterized by partnership. The spouses work together to create the kind of life that they see as worthwhile. In such a marriage, the happiness and love that we see are at least as much an outgrowth of the spouses' partnership as the origin of it.

In our society, we do not usually think of happiness as something that follows from commitment and teamwork. We want to pursue it directly. But happiness is an emotion, and all emotions, by their nature, are fleeting. Letting our hopes rest primarily on feelings that come and go is a recipe for an unstable marriage. Happiness, when we make it a goal in itself, is very elusive. Chasing happiness is a lot like trying to catch a feather that is floating in the air: when you grab for the feather, the very movement of your hand pushes it away; the feather is much easier to capture if you cup your hands and let it float into them. A marital partnership is like a pair of cupped hands, and marital happiness is more a by-product of shared experiences, mutual commitment, and joint pursuits than something the couple can reach out and grasp directly.

The kind of partnership I will describe in this book is much larger and deeper than the happiness it makes possible. Indeed, marriage itself is both more and less than we habitually think it is. Even though marriage may sometimes be less emotionally fulfilling and less passionate than the myth suggests it should be, it contains more substance and meaning than we usually see in it.

A Shared Vision of the Good Marriage

Having a partnership marriage sounds lovely, doesn't it? But a partnership makes sense only if the two people are involved in some shared project or trying to accomplish shared goals. One error in our emphasis on the emotional features of marriage is that we have come to see marriage as a relationship between two individuals, and so we have reduced the relationship to their interactions and to the feelings that they have for each other. But there is much more to most marriages than the spouses' feelings. Couples have goals and ideals that give their marriages purpose and meaning beyond emotions. In fact, our strongest feelings are tied to the progress and frustration we experience in trying to achieve the aims that define our lives.

There are many ways to define a good marriage, and we should not be limited to thinking only about emotional considerations. For example, Annette and Greg learned that they did not have to make their marriage follow the prewritten script of the dominant story of romance and emotional fulfillment. This realization helped them leave the fantasy behind and discover that their marriage had more in it of Annette and Greg than of the vague "happily ever after" dream. A good marriage can be built on the pursuit of any number of worthy goals: raising responsible children, undertaking community activities together, participating jointly in family or religious traditions, and developing some form of excellence, to name just a few. Although the specific characteristics of this shared life will be somewhat different for each couple, pursuing meaningful shared goals as a couple is central to a good marriage.

Virtue in Marriage

As I have observed many different couples, I have become convinced that strong marriages are built on the virtues or character strengths of the spouses. In other words, the best way to have a good marriage is to be a good person. Virtues are the character traits that help us live a good life and embody our ideals and aspirations. Practicing virtue is not about trying to be better than other people or denying ourselves enjoyment. When we act virtuously, we do our best to bring about something that we think is good, and we do it simply because we love the good.

Indeed, one of the things that strengthened Annette's and Greg's marriage was their having learned to practice the virtues that are essential to building a strong marriage. For example, when Greg sacrificed his free time to help Annette get an education, he did so gladly because he truly wanted the best for her and for their family. As they learned to overlook the negative in each other and emphasize the good, they gained a richer, more complex marital reality than they had thought possible. They found that they could forgive one another's irritating failings and even the significant hurts that they had inflicted on each other.

Chapters Six through Nine, in Part Two of this book, explore the role in marriage of four specific virtues: friendship, loyalty, generosity, and justice.

The virtue of *friendship* helps you foster a partnership marriage. Virtue or character friendships are created when we share a set of ideals about the good life with someone and we work together to embody those goals. Character friends also help each other flourish as individuals. Marriages that are based on character friendships are far richer and more durable than relationships founded on spouses' providing each other with pleasure or other benefits.

The virtue of *loyalty* helps you remain committed to your relationship in spite of the difficulties that inevitably arise over the course of a marriage. Loyalty is a powerful attachment that grows naturally out of participating in important relationships such as marriage, family, and nation. You can strengthen your marriage by cultivating this loyalty and acknowledging the bonds that you have forged with your partner through the shared joys and sorrows you experience in your everyday activities.

The virtue of *generosity* helps you overcome marriage's disagreements and hurts and come to terms with your partner's human foibles. Because we are all flawed and limited, generosity is a necessary component of a lifelong marriage. Generous spouses give freely to one another, forgive each other, and see the best in their partners.

Fairness or justice seems indispensable to a good marriage today. For this reason, the virtue of *justice* is very important to a good marriage. You can foster justice in your marriage by recognizing that your partner has different strengths and needs than you do and by finding a way to share the burdens and benefits of marriage as a couple. Justice in marriage is not just about redressing imbalances between men and women and splitting up tasks and goodies equally. It emerges when you shoulder the work and difficulties of the marriage together and when you share the joys of life *as a couple*.

Marriage and Belonging

Marriage is an important avenue for helping us find a meaningful place in the world by pursuing shared goals with a partner that tie us to our social world. For example, Annette and Greg have come to recognize that their lives—as spouses, as parents, and as active participants in their community—have become thoroughly intertwined. They see that they are not really separate individuals, joined only by love and choice; rather, as a result of their sharing so much of their lives, both of them have changed and grown. They have discovered that their shared life makes them part of each other and joins them more profoundly than romance ever could. The ideals that guide their lives come in part from their cultural backgrounds, are received in part from their families, and result in part from their own experiences and decisions. They have discovered the importance of their community in raising their children and in finding a place for themselves as a couple. Their shared projects take them beyond themselves as individuals and as a couple, drawing them into the life of their community.

The Crucible of Marriage

In a nutshell, then, this book is about how we can move beyond the myth of marital happiness by recognizing how to build strong marriages through partnerships devoted to a shared view of the good life. Working together toward common goals requires character strengths. In other words, one of the best ways to improve a marriage is to become a better person by cultivating and practicing such virtues as friendship, loyalty, generosity, and justice.

Once we recognize that our monotonous emphasis on the emotional payoffs of marriage captures only a small portion of what marriage is, a whole new vista opens up. We find that marriage provides a wonderful opportunity for us to transcend our narrow individual experiences and emotions. Although we choose a spouse on the basis of an emotional attachment, marriage gives us the chance to work with our chosen person to bring cherished aims and ideals to life. We can build on that attachment to form a deep bond of loyalty and friendship through which the marriage becomes a shared journey toward the accomplishment of goals that make our lives worth living. Indeed, we find that marriage is one of the best opportunities we have to develop our characters—to become the best people we can be.

2

The Magic Union

Americans tend to assume that feelings define love,
and that permanent commitment can come only from
having the proper clarity, honesty, and openness
about one's feelings.
Robert Bellah and others, Habits of the Heart[1]

In contemporary American culture, marriage is the centerpiece of our personal lives. Being in a happy marriage is the decisive factor in whether people feel happy with their lives as a whole. Although simply being married appears to be beneficial in itself, we place the real emphasis and value on marital happiness or satisfaction—how we feel about our relationships. We have exalted the emotional aspects of marriage so much that a marriage is good only if it feels good. Marriage has become, in Augustus Napier's words, "the magic union."[2]

The trouble is, at the same time that we have maximized our expectations for emotional fulfillment in marriage, we have minimized our sense of obligation and commitment to marriage. Divorce has become the natural response when our expectations for happiness in our marriages go unfulfilled. A widespread concern about the fragility of marriage and the negative effects of divorce has led many professionals, clergy, and politicians to look for ways to shore up marriage. There is a remarkable degree of agreement among experts, the popular press, and the public that good communication is the best solution to the instability of contemporary marriages. But is good communication enough to make our marriages strong and lasting?

In this chapter, I will show that our expectations for marital happiness are too extravagant, and that seeing good communication as the defining feature of a good marriage obscures some of the most significant aspects of marriage. Moreover, to believe that improving communication is the best way to strengthen a marriage is to pour gasoline on a fire because the real problem with marriage is that we expect too much from it already. Proposals to improve communication can actually inflame our expectations, leading us to believe that we really can get everything we want from marriage if only we can learn to communicate better.

The myth of marital happiness has narrowed the meaning of our marriages to how we feel about our relationships and to how we communicate with each other. This means that the entire relationship comes down to what happens between husband and wife. Our feelings and communication are important, but they are only two of many ways that we can experience the goodness in our marriages. As we will see in later chapters, the richness and depth of good marriages are built on shared goals and characterized by the loyalty that develops between partners who have shared important joys and sorrows in their married life.

Benefits of Marriage

How important is marital happiness? As I already mentioned, the emotional aspects of marriage are so compelling to us in contemporary America that we have made marital satisfaction the single most important factor in our overall personal happiness. For most people, it is more important to personal well-being than friends, jobs, religion, housing, or money. In fact, most studies show that the influence of marital quality is stronger than all these other sources of well-being combined.[3] For example, according to Joseph Veroff,

Elizabeth Douvan, and Shirley Hatchett, among the foremost researchers of psychological well-being in America, "in conducting research on the quality of life of the American population, time and again we came to the conclusion that for most adults the cornerstone of a solidly constructed life free from overwhelming tensions is a happy and stable marriage."[4] It is not clear how we as a culture could emphasize the emotional aspects of marriage more than we do.

The benefits of marriage can be measured in many ways that are more tangible and consequential than subjective impressions of personal happiness. Married individuals tend to be better off financially; wives as well as husbands earn substantially more as individuals than men and women who are not married.[5] Being married decreases your risk of illness and increases your longevity. Compared to married women, women the same age who are unmarried are 50 percent more likely to die, and single men are two and one-half times more likely to die than are married men of the same age. Unmarried people die earlier, largely because they are less likely to take good care of themselves. They are more likely to die from causes and conditions related to their behavior; examples are lung cancer, cirrhosis of the liver, suicide, and accidents.

If you are married, you are also much less likely to experience serious forms of mental illness, particularly anxiety and depression. Being married substantially reduces the risk of suicide, whereas divorce more than doubles that risk.[6] **This means that in contemporary America, the single most important thing you can do to enhance your physical and psychological well-being is to be happily married.**

Questions About the Benefits of Marriage

In *The Future of Marriage*, Jessie Bernard points out that men benefit more from marriage, psychologically and physically, than women do.[7] Her important qualification of the benefits of marriage is sometimes misinterpreted to mean that women do not benefit from marriage. In fact, however, women do benefit from marriage, in all the ways that men do. The difference is that marriage is merely good for women, whereas for men it is virtually lifesaving. Part of this disparity is due to the fact that single men's well-being is significantly lower than single women's in terms of physical and mental health, finances, and education. Therefore, men have a lot more to gain from marriage than women do.

You may wonder whether marriage confers these benefits or whether it is simply that healthier, more financially promising individuals are more likely to marry. (We know, for example, that individuals with serious mental or physical disabilities are less likely to marry.[8])

If we were only comparing people who marry with people who have never married, individual characteristics might explain the differences between them. But the personal characteristics of those who are divorced are the same as when they were married, and the traits of those who are remarried are the same as when they were divorced. An individual's characteristics don't change simply because he or she divorces or remarries. An individual's prospects for mental and physical health do change, however. Both married and remarried people are better off than single people are, regardless of whether single people have never married or are now divorced. Clearly, individual characteristics are not the whole story.

In addition, marriage contributes to personal health directly through social support, which is the assistance, caring, and involvement that people give one another in personal relationships, both materially and emotionally. Social support helps to explain why some people live longer, are healthier, and are less subject than others to psychological difficulties. In particular, it is important to have a readily available confidant, someone with whom you can really talk and on whom you can depend when life gets difficult. People consider their spouses their primary confidants far more often than they see their parents, siblings, adult children, or extended family members in this role.[9] When people are asked who provides them with the most social support and which relationships are most satisfactory, they rate their spouses and their marriages highest. Thus, because marriage is the single most important source of social support, we can see that marriage in itself is beneficial.

The Popularity of Marriage

Another way to recognize the importance of marriage in this country is by its popularity. Given all the benefits I just described, it is hardly surprising that marriage is an extremely popular institution in this country. About 96 percent of Americans say that they have a strong desire to marry, a figure that has not changed over the past thirty years, and about 90 percent of all adults do marry at least once. Indeed, Americans have one of the highest rates of marriage and remarriage in the world.[10]

A Retreat from Marriage?

For all the importance and allure of marriage, people now are less likely to marry and remarry than in the recent past. Just forty years ago, about 97 percent of adults married at least once, in contrast with the 90 percent who do so today. This recent decline is largely offset by the increasing popularity of cohabitation. More and more couples are choosing to live together without marrying. A sharp increase in cohabitation began to occur about 1970. Couples today are four times more likely to live together before marriage than they were just thirty years ago.[11] Four out of five people who live together expect to marry their partners. They often say that the most important reason they live together is to decide whether they will be compatible in marriage.

For most people, cohabitation is a stage of courtship. To some degree, living together is a response to anxiety about divorce. These individuals hope that cohabiting will help them decide more confidently whether to marry their partners. Living together is not generally a retreat from marriage or a repudiation of marriage. In fact, couples invest a great deal in their courtship by cohabiting, because it is an elaborate attempt to make marriage a better bet.

Unfortunately, those who marry after living together are actually somewhat more likely to divorce than those who do not. The longer a couple lives together before marriage, the more likely it is that the partners will divorce.[12] Those who cohabit exhibit an understandable skittishness about marriage. Ironically, their worries about being stuck in a bad marriage may also make them less likely to remain committed if the marriage proves difficult. This means that anxiety about having a happy marriage leads more people to cohabit, and it also increases their chances of divorce.

Desperately Seeking Marital Happiness

We can see the popularity of marriage even more clearly in the cycle of marriage, divorce, and remarriage. It would be easy to see the high rates of divorce in this country as a rejection of marriage. Ironically, however, divorce is one of the strongest affirmations of the importance of happiness in marriage. This affirmation shows up clearly in the fact that people generally say they got divorced because they could not have the close companionship with their spouses that they wanted.

In her fascinating book *Divorce Talk*, Catherine Reissman concludes, "Although this ideal vision of marriage . . . has failed them, women and men nevertheless affirm it by justifying their divorces on the grounds that particular core elements of the companionate ideal—emotional intimacy, primacy and companionship, and sexual fulfillment—were missing from their marriages." She goes on to say that none of the people she interviewed "questioned the ideology of the companionate marriage. It was the failure of their particular partners to live up to the ideal that was defined as the problem, not the dream itself."[13]

We can also see divorce as an affirmation of marriage in the fact that, for most people, divorce is actually a stage in the search for a satisfying relationship, given that more than three-quarters of those who divorce do eventually remarry. Most remarriages occur within three years of divorce, and the result is a remarriage rate that is higher in the United States than in other Western nations.[14]

These statistics are stunning because most divorced individuals have been deeply disappointed and hurt by their experience, but the wish to participate in a happy marriage is enough for them to shake off this negative outcome and try again. Remarriage is, as Samuel Johnson once said, the triumph of hope over experience. This is even truer today than when he said it because remarriages are even more likely than first marriages to end in divorce.[15]

Isn't it amazing how much people will go through in search of a satisfying marriage? The stakes are so high that couples are willing to substantially increase the complexity and length of courtship by living together. So important is the ideal of a happy marriage that many Americans are willing to marry, divorce, and remarry for its sake. The myth of marital happiness is powerful indeed. Let's look into what we want so desperately from our marriages and what inspires us to go to such extremes.

The Conventional Concept of a Good Marriage

In contemporary America, marriage is first and foremost about love. The most important expectation people have for their marriages is to experience love and affection. In spite of the increasing frequency of divorce, in the last thirty years companionship and emotional security have become even more important factors in marriage. Attractiveness, financial issues, class, race, educational level, and other personal characteristics play some role, of course, although most Americans disapprove of marriages based primarily on these kinds of considerations. Mutual love, as the outgrowth of our historical idealization of romance, stands as the primary reason to marry in our culture.[16]

When my wife, Susan, read this chapter, she reminded me that we, like most other parents and family members, will probably be very interested in the educational levels, incomes, and social standing of the mates our children choose. Most parents do want their children to be happy, of course, but love does not blind friends and family members to important practical realities. Susan is right, and her comment made it clear to me that it is one thing to cheer when, in a movie like *Pretty Woman*, a corporate raider and a prostitute fall in love and overcome their social and economic differences for the sake of love; it is something else again to face the prospect of your own children marrying either a corporate raider or a prostitute. This comparison shows the difference between the abstract notion of love conquering all and the ordinary reality of love and happiness as only two of many factors that are important in a good marriage.

Marital researchers, therapists, the media, and the public continue to express the contemporary cultural formula that feelings of love and satisfaction are the glue that keeps a marriage together. This viewpoint is seldom seriously questioned in either the professional or the popular literature. There are many different variations on this theme, but almost everyone takes these feelings for granted as the core of a good marriage. For example, in their recent book *The Good Marriage*, Judith Wallerstein and Sandra Blakeslee rhapsodize about these hopes:

> We want and need erotic love, sympathetic love, passionate love, tender, nurturing love all of our adult lives. We desire friendship, compassion, encouragement, a sense of being understood and appreciated, not only for what we do but for what we try to do and fail at. We want a relationship in which we can test our half-baked ideas without shame or pretense and give voice to our deepest fears. We want a partner who sees us as unique and irreplaceable.
>
> A good marriage can offset the loneliness of life in crowded cities and provide a refuge from the hammering pressures of the competitive work place. It can counter the anomie of an increasingly impersonal world, where so many people interact with machines rather than fellow workers. In a good marriage each person can find sustenance to ease the resentment we all feel about hav-

ing to yield to other people's wishes and rights. Marriage provides an oasis where sex, humor, and play can flourish.[17]

Wallerstein and Blakeslee suggest that the passion, intimacy, emotional support, and deep satisfaction of a good marriage can make up for virtually all the incessant, sometimes debilitating, demands of modern life. That is not too much to ask, now is it? But this is not just an idiosyncratic fantasy. You can find similar views throughout the professional and popular literature. Wallerstein and Blakeslee are simply expressing hopes and fantasies about marriage that are widespread in our culture. They provide a very clear statement of the common hope that a loving, companionate marriage can heroically overcome all the stress and alienation we endure in modern life. And yet I think their bold statement of this consensus helps us to see that this extravagant ideal may actually be larger than life.

For the most part, Americans define love in terms of feelings of physical and psychological attraction, intimacy, mutual support, enjoyment, and exclusivity. In our work with engaged and married couples, my research associates and I have heard these themes echoed repeatedly. The individuals with whom we have spoken say that they chose their mates as a result of the deep bond of love that emerged between them.

Carol, for example, a twenty-eight-year-old administrative assistant, describes in these terms what is good about her marriage with Andrew: "We love each other very much, and it is a great feeling. I feel a lot of support from him. He is there for me always. He loves me in a way nobody ever has. I have never felt so loved in my life, and it helps me feel really good about myself."

Matt, a thirty-one-year-old computer technician, also expresses deep love for his wife, Angela. In response to our question about what is good in his marriage, he says, "I like the love I feel for her. This isn't my first marriage, and I have never felt like this before with a woman. I feel committed, and I feel like I will enjoy, love, and cherish Angela just as much forty years from now as I do today. I just love who she is. She is just incredible. This is a completely new feeling for me, and I am just hopelessly in love with her."

Spontaneous Belonging

Virtually all the couples with whom we have talked make a point of telling their stories of courtship, framing it as a relatively easy, natural evolution from acquaintanceship or friendship to a committed marriage. They speak of feeling at home with each other, and of this feeling having led to the recognition that getting married just felt natural and right. In one way or another, almost all of them say that the freedom to be themselves with their partners was a key component of the "rightness" in the decision to marry. In *Habits of the Heart*, Robert Bellah and his colleagues say that a spouse will often describe his or her relationship as "so spontaneous that it carries a powerful sense of inevitability"; the relationship feels so natural that it promotes a deep sense of belonging, "a sense that the self has found its right place in the world."[18]

Matt, the computer technician married to Angela, describes the development of his relationship as a natural progression: "When we started dating, we saw each other a couple of times a week. Gradually, we got together more often, then we spent some weekends together, and then we took a trip together. Every time we spent more time together, the relationship felt more and more right. Then we moved in together, and, I don't know, there was just a time when it was clear to me that nothing was going to happen to end this relationship." Their decision to marry emerged as natural and unforced over the course of the year they had known each other.

Even when the decision takes time, however, or when there are serious obstacles and the relationship does not develop smoothly from the initial meeting to marriage, couples still describe the deepening of the relationship as a natural progression toward commitment. Often these individuals portray the decision to marry less as a choice than as a recognition of what the relationship has already become.

For example, Tom, a tall, serious carpenter, explains his decision to marry Marie: "I just knew that this was the woman I wanted to spend the rest of my life with." Tom and Marie met through a work setting and became friends. In the beginning, he was unsure whether he dared to ask her out. He talked to some friends, and they encouraged him. "Once we started dating, things seemed to happen real quickly. We were so comfortable, and it felt so right. It was like we were really good friends, and it just turned into best friends, and everything clicked, and everything happened. It seemed quick, but we talked about it a lot. Everything just seemed right. It did not seem rushed, and it seemed like we belonged together."

Marie also highlights the importance of being friends first, which she sees as the best way to begin a relationship: "We were friends first, and I never thought that he would be the person I would end up marrying, and we ended up getting extremely close, and it was just like one day we both turned around and went, Gee, we really love each other, don't we? You know, everything else fell into place after that."

It is not hard to see why this vision of spontaneous, mutual love is so enticing. As we will see, however, it has serious pitfalls.

The Communication Formula for a Good Marriage

From my conversations with the couples in my studies, with couples in therapy, with students, and with others, communication emerges as a critical element in romantic relationships. If you were to ask just about anyone what it takes to have a good marriage, almost anyone would say that communication is the key. Sharing our thoughts and feelings is indispensable to emotional intimacy because this kind of communication provides the possibility for us to discover more about each other and grow as a couple. Feeling free to share ourselves fully is one of the deepest aspirations Americans have for modern love relationships. Ideally, a spouse is someone who can hear and share your joys and sorrows, triumphs and anxieties, hopes and feelings of desperation. I have been struck by how fervently people believe that listening, understanding, and responding to one another's needs is the primary way that we renew our marital bonds.

Wallerstein and Blakeslee highlight the contemporary centrality of nurturing communication: "The main task of every marriage from the early days of the relationship to its end is for each partner to nurture the other. The loneliness of life in cities, the long commutes, the absence of meaningful contact with people have all sharpened our emotional hungers. More than ever before, we need someone special who understands how we feel and responds with tenderness. A marriage that does not provide nurturance and restorative comfort can die of emotional malnutrition."[19]

Because we seek romantic love and psychological intimacy, communication is indispensable: it creates the possibility of our knowing and appreciating our partners as individuals. The spouses we have interviewed place a great deal of stress on this mutual discovery and on how their relationships have become more meaningful as the partners have come to understand each other better. In fact, virtually none of the people in my studies say that their marriages are happy unless they feel that they have good communication; and if they think that they communicate well, then they almost certainly feel satisfied with their relationships. Social scientists actually have a difficult time separating what people say about marital communication from what people say about marital satisfaction.[20]

This bonding of communication, love, and satisfaction also shows up in how partners talk about their relationships. Helene, whom we met in Chapter One as the daycare worker married to Kevin, feels that "communication is the most important thing. If you can't communicate, then you can exist together, but it wouldn't be a marriage. It would be just an existence, so communication is the core of the marriage. I think that open communication is being able to tell [Kevin] everything, or being able to tell him what I really feel. If something bothers me now, I know that I can go to Kevin and tell him, whatever it is. I've been married before, and that's why it's so important, because I didn't feel like I could talk to my ex-husband. I didn't want to talk to him—I didn't think that he could understand—whereas with Kevin, I know that even if he doesn't understand, even if he doesn't agree, he will take it in, and he will at least try to accept it and work with me, and I try to do that with him. That's where I think that communication is the willingness to see the other person's point of view."

According to Howard Markman, Scott Stanley, and Susan Blumberg, authors of *Fighting for Your Marriage*, this ability to hear the other person out and acknowledge the communication, even when you disagree, is a highly valued component of how we see good communication. These authors describe what spouses said about what they wanted in their relationships: "What do you think they told us? Financial security? No. Good sex? No. Emotional security? No. The major desire people have is for their partner to be a friend. When we ask, 'What is a friend?' people tell us that a friend is someone who listens, who understands, who validates."[21] Many people with whom I have talked go even farther: what they want in a spouse is not just a friend but a *best* friend.

Happiness, Communication, and the Fragility of Marriage

We all know, of course, that many couples do not experience this spontaneous, unproblematic emotional bond, but most of us want our relationships to have that character. And when there are important difficulties in our relationships, we believe that communication becomes even more crucial.

Communication and Its Discontents

When a couple is having problems, the partners usually characterize them as communication problems. Virtually all the people I have helped with marital difficulties began therapy by saying that they just could not communicate with their spouses. This usually meant that they were unable to resolve the conflicts they were experiencing, and that they were unable to share with each other in a way that continued to nurture their love relationship.

Sonia, for example, a no-nonsense middle manager in the cellular telephone industry, has been married once before and feels that she is going into her second marriage with a clearer sense of what is important to her. She wants her spouse to be her best friend, "someone who is going to open up to me and will let me open up to him." She decided to marry Anthony because she feels that he is her best friend. She says, "I can tell him everything, everything that happens to me, how I feel, things I like, things I do not like. I am really honest."

At the same time, Sonia has some concerns about the relationship, and they center on her feeling that Anthony is not as communicative as she would like him to be. Because communication is so central to her understanding of love, Anthony's reluctance to be fully open with her hurts her feelings, and she worries that he may not truly care about her. Anthony, for his part, is unambiguously committed to marrying Sonia, and he expresses his love for her in many different ways. But his loving behavior is not enough to alleviate Sonia's anxiety, because love, for her, is fully believable only when it is expressed through open, spontaneous communication.

One consequence of the belief that communication is so important in our relationships is that many of us, like Sonia, do not recognize other acts of love if the communication that we idealize is lacking. For example, I worked in marital therapy with a professional couple, Don and Cindy, who began with a major unresolved conflict about whether they should have children. Don had been married before, and he had two grown children from that marriage. He thought that he had done as much parenting as he wanted to do. He knew that having children would distract him and Cindy from their relationship and that it would add many complications to the comfortable life he had in mind. Cindy was much younger, and this was her first marriage. Although she had initially agreed not to have children, she later felt that her desire for them was too strong for her to forgo this experience.

Don and Cindy came to therapy after the birth of a child—an event due to a "mistake" in birth control. (Cindy's unsuccessful practice of birth control was, of course, a major point of contention.) They had been in conflict for months about this issue, and their negative feelings about the disagreement had begun to color their relationship to such an extent that they were beginning to consider divorce.

Two things struck me in my initial meeting with this couple. First, I found them both extremely likable, reasonable, decent people who had many personal strengths. As they told their story, it was hard to see how they could be as negative and adamant with each other as they described. Second, it was completely obvious to me that they loved each other very much and were both deeply committed to their relationship, but they believed themselves to be at a hopeless impasse.

As a result of this conflict, they had lost sight of their love for each other and of their commitment to their relationship. But it was very easy for me, as an outsider, to see their love for and commitment to each other, and I commented on it. They both reacted to my reflection of their personal strengths, and of the strength of their relationship, with tears and with a sense of connection and hope, which they had not felt in many weeks. This was only the beginning of therapy for this couple, but it reestablished a context of commitment and shared goals (apart from childrearing) and was an essential first step.

What is most significant is that these two likable, caring people could not recognize their love for and commitment to each other, because it was not apparent in their communication. As long as they focused only on their communication, they felt despair at the impasse in their relationship. Their inability to experience harmony in their communication caused them to worry that they no longer loved each other, and their inability to work out their differences through communication prevented them from seeing the other aspects of their relationship that were good. They lost sight of the strengths in their relationship because the premium they placed on communication made their disagreements the most important aspect of their marriage.

Their disagreement about having children (and even about Cindy's "betrayal" with birth control) was substantial, but as they gradually reclaimed the solidity and depth of their relationship, they saw that their differences could be worked out—largely because the relationship meant so much to them, and thanks to their mutual commitment and the shared life they had built.

The Inevitability of Miscommunication

One thing I have learned in fourteen years of marriage is that some degree of miscommunication and conflict is inevitable. My wife and I love each other very much, and we make every effort to communicate well. Even so, Susan and I are different people with different backgrounds, and we have different desires at times. Some of our miscommunications happen again and again. Each of us, at times, has despaired when we have had difficulty talking to each other or working out our disagreements.

Susan and I have gradually learned that our miscommunications are due partly to our differences and partly to our simply being human. Because we, too, are influenced by the cultural belief that communication is central to marriage, we have often worried that having occasional or even regular problems in communication signals a serious problem in our relationship. But when we look at the big picture of our relationship—the attachment that has grown through our shared joys and suffering, the mutual commitment we have to our goals and ideals, and the love, respect, and admiration we have for each other—the quality of our communication no longer looks like the only indicator of the quality of our marriage.

For many marriages, the professional and popular emphasis on communication can be helpful. If we focus too much on communication, however, we risk two consequences.

First, by narrowing our cultural understanding of a good marriage so much that spouses only feel positive about their relationship if they communicate well, they may disregard other positive features of their marriage, such as their shared history and mutual goals.

Second, our preoccupation with satisfaction and communication leads us to expect too much from marriage. Given the stresses and strains of contemporary life, the idealized communication that is so widely promoted frequently requires superhuman effort. But that is not all. Conflicts over differences in personal preferences and needs are actually more likely to occur than ever before. These conflicts are more powerful now than in the past because marriage has become the primary arena in which we seek to get our emotional needs and desires fulfilled. Conflict in our marriages is consequently more important and painful now than ever before because marital happiness has become so critical to our well-being.

Marital Happiness and Conditional Commitment

The idea that abiding love is the key to a lasting marriage appears indispensable to us, for several reasons. The most important reason is that it helps to preserve our sense of autonomy while allowing for a kind of ongoing commitment. As Robert Bellah and his coauthors put it, "Americans are . . . torn between love as an expression of spontaneous inner freedom, a deeply personal, but necessarily somewhat arbitrary, choice, and the image of love as a firmly planted, permanent commitment, embodying obligations that transcend the immediate feelings or wishes of the partners in a love relationship."[22] They discuss two approaches to marriage: the "traditional" approach, which is founded more on obligation, and the more dominant "therapeutic" approach, which emphasizes communication and satisfaction.

The traditional version of marriage is found primarily among Christian evangelical and other fundamentalist religious groups. Although love is important in these unions, it is secondary to obligation. For these couples, love is more a matter of will and action than of feelings. From this point of view, we love through engaging in caring, beneficent action rather than through internally experienced feelings. Many of these couples seek the same kind of communication and intimacy that others want, but they do so within a framework of duty and commitment.

As Bellah and his coauthors point out, however, most Americans are not willing to accept marriage as an indissoluble commitment: our overriding investment in individual freedom makes unconditional commitment virtually impossible. Many of us recoil at the thought of having duties or obligations that transcend our personal choices. If we are to feel truly free to live our own lives, we think we must be free to alter or terminate our commitments as we see fit, and binding commitments are incompatible with this kind of freedom.

The therapeutic approach to marriage is an attempt to overcome the incompatibility between individual freedom and binding commitments. The premise of the therapeutic approach is that if we can maintain our feeling of love for our spouses, and our freely given attachment to them, then we can preserve our freedom because we will remain committed through our own desire, not through constraint. To the extent that we find belonging, intimacy, and nurturance in marriage, we feel that the relationship is meeting our individual needs, and our continued commitment to the relationship is consistent with the freedom to pursue our personal aims. In the absence of this fulfillment of our needs, commitment seems like an unreasonable burden that is difficult to justify.

For example, Matt, the computer technician we met earlier, very clearly expresses his opinion that the proper order is for commitment to follow one's feelings: "It was clear to me that Angela was feeling the same way as I was, and we talked about marriage together. I didn't just pop the question to her. We felt that the relationship was permanent, and we felt committed to each other first, and then it made sense to get married. We didn't get married to make it permanent and committed. I already felt permanent and committed, and that made it time to get married. I think that is the right way to do it. It is more like a natural growth instead of being forced and artificial."

Is Happiness Everything in Marriage?

Marital happiness is important. We do not need to give it up as one important indicator of the quality of a marriage. But I am suggesting that it is only one of many ways to recognize the goodness in our marriages.

Some years ago, I worked with a couple, Wendy and Al, who taught me something about going beyond communication, intimacy, and happiness in marriage. I have never forgotten what this couple taught me. They came to see me as a last resort before seeking a divorce. They had been married for twenty years and felt that their relationship had become hollow and meaningless. They saw no reason to continue being married unless they could develop some warmth and intimacy in their relationship. Increasing their intimacy seemed like a reasonable goal to me as well, so I set about helping them improve their communication and develop greater emotional closeness.

I found that they both would talk to me about how they felt about each other, rather than talking directly to each other. As long as they talked to me rather than to each other, their emotional intimacy would not increase. They might come to know more about each other, but they would not feel more connected.

Using a common (and commonsensical) strategy among marital therapists, I suggested that they talk directly to each other. My suggestion scared them half to death, and they were very reluctant to follow it. I coached them in expressing themselves, and at times

I helped translate what they were saying to each other. We persisted, and they gradually learned to communicate better. Eventually they were able to converse with each other normally, although they still could not really share their feelings directly with each other or ask for what they wanted from each other without my help. But they did come to terms with important aspects of their past that were getting in the way, and they worked out some difficulties in parenting their children.

I felt good about these successes, but it was also true that Wendy and Al did not seem to be developing the deep intimacy and fully open communication I thought they wanted. After they had been meeting with me over the course of several months, they told me that they were going to start a business marketing Native American art together. They both had an abiding interest in this artwork and in helping to maintain certain Native American art forms. I reflected that this project seemed to represent a renewed form of their commitment to each other. They happily agreed and talked with enthusiasm about the project.

Several weeks later, they began thanking me for my help and telling me that they thought they were finished in therapy. I was a little surprised, although I did not express my surprise overtly, and even disappointed because we had not really met their initial goal of deeper emotional intimacy. Nevertheless, they told me that they believed their relationship was much stronger. Their judgment about feeling finished with therapy was more important than mine was, of course, and so we wrapped up by summarizing what we had accomplished together, and I wished them well.

Gradually, it has become clear to me that they found another way besides deepening intimacy to have a good marriage. Their way involved joint participation in a project that gave their marriage a deeper and more lasting meaning than emotional intimacy could by itself. Their business partnership connected them with thousands of years of tradition and allowed them to share an abiding passion for art with each other and with other people. This shared project and its connection to larger concerns transcended and shaped their emotional experience and solidified their relationship. In other words, they gave their marriage a new dimension by working toward some common goals in their business. Their relationship was no longer just about what occurred in their personal interactions; it also included their working together to pursue a shared project that they both thought was important.

Wendy and Al taught me that marriage can be a *partnership* that transcends emotion in some ways. The therapy helped them work out some of their problems, and it seemed to clear the way for them to renew their commitment to each other and undertake this joint project. Their relationship did improve when they learned to talk to each other again, but their connection to each other was made far stronger by their passionate pursuit of a common interest. **Being able to communicate in an open and positive manner is very valuable, but having something worthwhile to communicate about is at least as important.** Their feelings for each other were enhanced by their excitement about their shared project.

Feeling happy and intimate with each other was no longer the ultimate aim of their marriage. Happiness and intimacy, although still important, were more the by-products of their ability to work together than the ultimate goal of their relationship. They showed me that there is more than one way to have a good marriage, and that we are not limited to the dominant cultural story of happiness as the only indicator of a strong marriage.

Of course, I will not be recommending that every couple start a business together. Instead, I will share many different projects that have helped couples to enhance their marriages. These examples can help you recognize and build on the strengths and other sources of goodness in your marriage and can help you be less dependent on the inconstancy of emotion as the sole barometer of having a good marriage.

3

How Did We Get Here?

A Brief History of a Myth

For there is no creature whose inward being is so strong that it is not greatly determined by what lies outside it.

George Eliot, Middlemarch[1]

We have seen that our romantic, satisfaction-oriented approach to marriage has created serious difficulties for us. How did we get into such a mess?

Marriage has not always been so fragile, which means that the explanation for the paradox of marriage must be historical. Although I find the story of marriage over the past five hundred years absolutely fascinating, I know that not everyone shares my passion for history. Therefore, let me give you the conclusions of this chapter first. You can then decide whether to read the rest of the chapter and get the details or simply skip ahead, having gained a basic understanding of the evolution of marriage.

In the Middle Ages, marriage was primarily an economic and political union, usually arranged by the fathers of the bride and the groom and closely supervised by the clan and the neighbors. There was little privacy, nor was there much expectation for emotional fulfillment in marriage.

Gradually, and with the encouragement of the church, people gained more say in whom they would marry. The reasons for marriage slowly shifted, from serving the family's economic and political interests to serving the individual's ends by marrying on the basis of mutual affection and, eventually, romantic love. As marriage became more love-oriented, the privacy of the couple and sexual fulfillment grew in importance, and as individual satisfaction with marriage became paramount, restrictions on divorce were progressively relaxed, until no-fault divorce laws were enacted.

This historical trajectory teaches us that we can trace the shifts from one form of marriage to another. There is a logic in this development, and the history even seems to contain elements of progress. But we can also see that the paradoxical combination of marriage's importance and its fragility was not historically necessary. More important, by recognizing that marriage has changed so much, we cannot help seeing that it will continue to change. This means that we are not trapped in the currently dominant story of marriage and that the search for better alternatives for creating stronger marriages can be very fruitful. If I have piqued your interest in the historical twists and turns of marriage, read on. If you feel that you know as much as you want to about this history, feel free to skip to the next chapter.

A priest named Lambert wrote the *History of the Counts of Guines* between 1201 and 1206 C.E. He gives us a marvelous look at marriage among the aristocracy in medieval France, and he illustrates how much marriage has changed over the centuries.

When the future Count Baldwin II was a young boy, his father matched him with an heiress. His prospective bride was brought before a large audience in her father's house, was informed of this match, and "expressed her willingness by the happy expression of her face." This was enough to indicate her consent to the marriage, and all in attendance acclaimed the betrothal. The couple was married some years later and had ten children.

Years later, Count Baldwin's eldest son, Arnulf, became betrothed to a daughter of the Count of Saint-Pol. Arnulf's betrothal to Saint Pol's daughter was broken when the only surviving son of Lord Bourbourg died, so that a much more advantageous marriage could be arranged with Lord Bourbourg's daughter, now the heiress. The first betrothal was cancelled fairly easily; dispensations were obtained from the Bishop of Thérouanne and the Archbishop of Reims. The future spouses indicated their consent to the marriage, and the bride was handed over to the husband's family, along with her dowry.

The wedding ceremony took place at night, in the couple's bedroom. When the couple had gone to their bed, Lambert and his sons, also priests, entered the room to sprinkle the couple with holy water and circle the bed with a censer. The priests blessed the newlyweds and committed them to God's keeping. At that point, Count Baldwin completed the ceremony. He raised his hands to heaven and asked God to bless his children, "joined together in holy copulation, and by the rites of marriage," so they would be steadfast in harmony and "their seed [would] be multiplied."[2] Baldwin then gave his own blessing to the couple.

The wedding ceremony was centered in the couple's bedroom because a wedding was, at that time, a domestic celebration and a prelude to the consummation of the marriage. After all, a primary purpose of the marriage was the production of an heir for the House of Guines because the future of the House depended on there being an heir. The next morning, three days of games and feasting began. This was to impress upon the guests the importance of the marriage and its consummation.

Two Models of Medieval Marriage

Not exactly romantic, is it? Marriage has certainly changed in the last few centuries, and the story of Count Baldwin II and his son illustrates many of the ways in which marriage today would be barely recognizable to those who lived in the Middle Ages. There was a deep tension in medieval society between the secular (and particularly the aristocratic) approach to marriage and the religious idea of marriage. This tension was one aspect of the political struggle between secular and religious powers that helped to shape Western society.[3] It may surprise you to learn how much this tension contributed to the form of marriage that we practice today. Let's begin our exploration of the fascinating twists and turns in the history of marriage with the conflict between the religious and secular models of marriage.

The Secular Model

Among families that had any property (farmers and shopkeepers included), the fathers of prospective couples arranged their marriages. In medieval times, marriage was less a personal relationship between two individuals than a treaty between two houses that was frequently made when the bride and bridegroom were children. The Christian church had succeeded, at this point, in establishing the custom that the future spouses must consent to the marriage, but, as we saw with Baldwin's future bride, the slightest sign was often taken as consent. By contrast with our times, love was not important in the selection process, even though it could grow between the spouses after the wedding.

Among the propertied classes, marriage was above all a mechanism for preserving or enhancing the property and standing of the family. The current head of the household was not so much its owner as a steward. He received the "house" from his father, and it was his duty to care for it and pass it on to his son, with a rank at least equal to his own when he himself had received it. In the interests of the house, a husband even had the right to repudiate (divorce) his wife if she failed to produce an heir, if she committed adultery, or if a more favorable match became available.

In the medieval world, society was built on the framework of kinship. A person was first and foremost a member of a particular family and clan, which provided a place within the larger society and imposed certain obligations and duties. The kinship group expected loyalty, and it actively supervised each individual's life to see that he or she acted in accordance with the accepted duties.

The lord's duty of open hospitality led to the presence of crowds of servants, retainers, and guests in the house. Houses in this period did not have hallways, and so there was very little privacy because people had to move about the house by passing through the rooms along the way. Husbands and wives had separate bedrooms and separate servants. Spouses were rarely together in private, and they did not expect or find much emotional intimacy in their marriages. The public solemnization of the marriage in the couple's bedroom denoted the family's interest in the production of an heir and symbolized the involvement of kin and community in the most intimate aspects of the couple's life.[4]

Although less wealthy spouses were not separated within the household by separate rooms and servants, their leisure activities were nevertheless segregated. The correspondence of the day shows that some degree of affection, or at least a good working partnership, developed between some spouses, but romantic love was rarely expressed. Partly because people did not expect very much from their marriages, arranged unions did not work out as badly as our romantic ideas about marriage would lead us to expect.

The Religious Model

Marriage was incredibly informal in the Middle Ages and it was often solemnized simply by two people's statement that they agreed to be married. There was no requirement of witnesses, ceremonies, or anyone else's consent. Among families with property, parents could influence the choice of a mate through the withholding of an inheritance, but among the poor there was little to prevent people from choosing their own spouses. The children of these families usually left home between the ages of seven and fourteen to enter domestic or agricultural service. But parental consent was still very important at this time, and children sought it ardently. If their parents were unavailable because of death or geographic distance, prospective spouses sought the approval of relatives, friends, or neighbors and often cancelled a marriage if approval was not forthcoming.

This amazingly fluid boundary between personal and public life is a striking characteristic of the European family up to the early sixteenth century. Communities actually exercised oversight of marriages at that time. Although the Catholic Church did not require the presence of a priest until 1563, and although priests were seldom even involved in marriage ceremonies, the church did manage to require couples to announce their betrothals before marriage (in a procedure known as the *banns of matrimony*). Once a betrothal was announced, the community became impatient if the marriage was not solemnized within a reasonable time. In one English diocese, for example, more than one hundred breach-of-promise cases were brought to court *by the community*, to prosecute couples who were betrothed but had not married. The community actually brought more breach-of-promise cases to court than jilted lovers did![5]

Neighbors gossiped about the intimate details of other families' lives, and they brought many complaints about the violation of community and religious standards to courts operated by the church. They complained of many matters, including the sleeping arrangements of servants in households, excessive cruelty to wives, and even the unusually enthusiastic sexual behavior of husbands and wives. They also avidly sought to discover adultery and bigamy among their neighbors and report it to the authorities.

The church gradually obtained jurisdiction over marriage through ecclesiastic courts. This development allowed the church to institute reforms, establish rules, and regulate marriage according to Catholic doctrine. The elaboration of a Christian model of marriage was one of the most important aspects of this change. Because the celibacy-minded church abhorred sexuality, it portrayed marriage as a means of keeping sexual activity controlled and directed for purposes of procreation only. The church gradually brought the wedding ceremony under religious control by moving it out of the house, to the door of the church and eventually into the church itself. Marriage eventually became one of the seven sacraments.

Religious leaders had long been unhappy with the practice of repudiating wives, and they worked to eliminate it. After centuries of debate and uncertainty, the Council of Trent proclaimed, in the 1560s, the Catholic doctrine that marriage could not be dissolved. A valid marriage could be ended only by the death of one of the spouses. Annulments were possible, but there were very few petitions for them, and the courts demanded rigorous evidence in order to grant them. The prohibition of divorce was the first revolution in divorce law; virtually all pre-Christian codes of law had allowed divorce.

The Beginnings of Affectionate Marriage

It is interesting that it was church leaders who led the way to making affection an important part of marriage. Their goal was to sanctify marriage by making the relationship between husband and wife more like the relationship between Christ and the church. The consent of bride and groom to the marriage was one step in this direction. The affection the church leaders had in mind was not the romantic love we idealize today. In fact, people in the Middle Ages took the idea of being "madly in love" quite literally: if you allowed yourself to be carried away by love, you would be ridiculed as a weak, immature individual. Public derision kept both the aristocracy and the peasantry from this foible. Among the poor, the *chivari*, a ritual public humiliation conducted by neighbors and kin, was used to correct a husband who, because of his overweening love for his wife, failed to maintain his preeminence over her. The community expected husbands to exhibit a benevolent, condescending love for the wives they had to protect, and wives were expected to have a respectful devotion to their husbands.

Historians do not make the absurd claim that romantic love did not exist in our history. For example, an Elizabethan watching *Romeo and Juliet* would be familiar enough with the captivating passion of love to feel some sympathy with the young lovers. But he would see the tragedy of their story less as a social injustice that had doomed their star-crossed love than as the lovers' having brought destruction on themselves by violating social custom. He would clearly see that duty and rationality precluded any romance that would lead him into such a plight.[6]

As late as the seventh century, people generally married for economic or political interest (although some degree of mutual affection was nevertheless desirable). In his diary, for example, Samuel Sewall, a seventeenth-century New England Puritan, describes marriage primarily as a property arrangement rather than an emotional bond. He prides himself on his success at making good financial settlements for his children's marriages. After his first wife's death, he pursues a succession of widows, and although his correspondence with them is somewhat concerned with personal feelings, it is far more concerned with the financial arrangements of a potential marriage.[7]

The balance between economic and romantic motives began to shift in the seventeenth century in England and, later, on the Continent, although romantic love and lust were still roundly condemned as temporary, irrational states unlikely to lead to a stable marriage. We play down economic interests in marriage today, but it is easy to see that most people marry someone with a similar level of education, similar income, and a similar class background. Thus it is not so much that marriage in earlier times was solely commercial, and that modern marriage is solely emotional; rather, over the course of our history there has been a shift in the balance between the factors of commerce and emotion. The important difference between our time and earlier times is that for us romantic love has become crucial to what makes married life worthwhile and significant.

I am presenting these changes in simplified form for the sake of brevity. The evolution of marriage proceeded in fits and starts, and the changes that occurred were often more prevalent in one country or social class than in others. Much of the time there was considerable contention and confusion about how marriage should be arranged and how married life should be lived. Nevertheless, there is a clearly discernible shift, away from a more distant, deferent, patriarchal, kinship-oriented medieval marriage and toward the more affectionate, egalitarian, private modern marriage.

Godly Love in Marriage

Just at the point where the Catholic Church seemed to be enjoying a triumph in the regulation of marriage, the Protestant Reformation burst on the scene. The Protestant Reformers reversed Catholic doctrine almost completely. They rejected the Catholic doctrines of the superiority of celibacy and of marriage as a sacrament. The Reformers taught that marriage is sanctified by the companionship of the spouses. Catholic doctrine stressed celibacy as a higher calling, and marriage as the best that ordinary mortals could do to contain their sexuality. In contrast, Protestant leaders proclaimed that marriage is actually better than celibacy. In their vision, marriage was in fact the best way of life.[8]

Protestant ministers continually extolled a more affectionate, mutually supportive bond between spouses, one that would sanctify marriage and make it *holy* matrimony. Marriages arranged to benefit the family economically or politically were severely criticized by the Reformers. Archbishop Cranmer officially added a third reason for marriage to the ancient motives of procreation and the avoidance of fornication. In his *Prayer Book* of 1549, he encouraged the spouses to give each other mutual support and comfort.[9]

A love-based marriage is less subject to social standards than a hierarchical marriage is. Therefore, love relationships allow less interference after the marriage, and the couple bonded in mutual affection can more easily present a united front to the world. Thus the increasing emphasis on the nuclear family of husband, wife, and children created a bond of affection and loyalty that competed with and undermined individuals' bonds to their kin.

As the basis for choosing a spouse shifted from economic and political factors to mutual affection, parents had less and less to say about whom their children would marry. This protracted social confusion about who was to pick a spouse, and about why two people should marry, is illustrated in the story of Simonds D'Ewes, a financially independent lawyer who was seeking marriage with a landed heiress in order to enhance his status.[10] But Simonds needed his father's consent to marry an heiress, for custom required his father to pledge a financial settlement on behalf of the bride should Simonds die. His father in turn wanted Simonds to marry a rich man's daughter, for a cash dowry would then, by custom, come to him as the groom's father. Simonds proposed two heiresses, whom his father refused, and his father proposed two daughters of rich merchants, whom Simonds rejected. Simonds turned down a promising bride, a wealthy heiress, because he found her unattractive.

Simonds was finally engaged to a suitably wealthy and attractive thirteen-year-old. She was too young to marry, but he visited her frequently, and their mutual affection grew. They married and remained devoted to each other. This story nicely illustrates the remaining importance of money and position, the power struggle between parents and children about the choice of mate, the emerging importance of mutual affection, and the son's ability to veto arrangements for reasons of financial interest or personal preference.

The Reappearance of Divorce

The Protestant Reformers rejected marriage as a sacrament because it had no scriptural basis, and marriage was not necessary for salvation. This rejection led almost immediately to the second divorce revolution: the legalization of divorce in all the Protestant states except England. (The English also managed to suppress divorce laws in all the American colonies except Massachusetts and Connecticut.) The Reformers worked out their doctrines of marriage and divorce slowly, with difficulty, and with great reluctance. They abandoned the indissolubility of marriage with less zest than they had done with other Catholic doctrines. The Reformers took marriage very seriously, and they allowed divorce only as a last resort. They made every effort to reconcile the spouses.

When the Protestant leaders rejected marriage as a sacrament, marriage once again became a contract. This was a momentous change because contracts are voluntary and can be broken when the conditions of the agreement are not being met by one or both parties. The changes in divorce law that came throughout Western societies over the next four centuries were possible only because of this shift from the biblical theory to the natural law theory of marriage, leading to the idea that marriage is a civil contract regulated by secular laws.

If marriage is a contract, a question arises: What are the spouses contracting *for*? Roderick Phillips, in his fascinating history of divorce, *Putting Asunder*,[11] points out that expectations of marriage at any given time are revealed by the conditions in which divorce is allowed. If a spouse violates these conditions, he or she voids the marriage contract.

Protestant leaders generally saw the marriage contract in terms of an acceptable outlet for sexuality, of procreation, and of the provision of companionship and support. In general, they allowed divorce only when one spouse violated one of these three purposes through adultery or desertion. The Reformers saw these offenses more as violations of the marriage contract than as injuries to the spouse. Divorce was not a solution for marital breakdown; rather, it was a punishment for a crime against marriage. Nevertheless, despite the permissibility of divorce, it was relatively rare before the nineteenth century.

Phillips illustrates Protestant divorce doctrine with Martin Luther's advice on a case of desertion. Luther advised a pastor to make every effort to locate a husband who had deserted his wife seven years earlier and to attempt to bring him back to his wife. Luther wanted an inquiry with neighbors to determine whether the wife had driven her husband away through her behavior. If she was innocent and her husband could not be induced to return, then her divorce petition could be granted. This story shows that divorce was a last resort to be granted as a remedy to this wife only if she was not implicated in the marital crime of desertion.

Even though affection was becoming more important, marriage remained an economic partnership for the vast majority of people at this time. It linked the family to a wider network of economic and social relationships. These marriages embodied a solidity and a unity that we find somewhat difficult to grasp today. For the vast majority of people, literally everything depended on marriage: their personal survival, the survival of their property, the survival of their posterity, and their place in the community. Traditional legal marriages created a unity that went beyond the spouses' individual interests. The partnership was based on the idea that the spouses were engaged in a joint enterprise, that they were responsible for each other, and that they would prosper or perish by virtue of their united efforts.[12]

This ideal of partnership and shared aims can help us renew marriage today. We would not want to revert to the male dominance of that time, but equal partnership is an ideal that could help us reverse the excessive emphasis on the separate interests of husbands and wives, an emphasis that makes our marriages so fragile.

Reemergence of the Secular Model

Affection was essential to Protestant theology because it made marriage holy—an end in itself—and it served as a bulwark against adultery. The importance of an affectionate relationship was related more to religious conceptions of marriage than to the enjoyment of the spouses in the seventeenth and eighteenth centuries. Gradually, over the course of the next two centuries, the attachment to religious ideology loosened, and the emotional tie between the spouses began to take on a life of its own and to become the primary end of marriage.

The Growth of Individualism

The gradual development of individualism was the most important change among the many twists and turns in the history of marriage. The growth of individualism entailed greater emphasis on personal autonomy, personal happiness, privacy in the family, warm emotional relations between husband and wife, and equality between the spouses. The rise of individualism meant a stronger preference for personal freedom over authority, an inclination toward spontaneity and affection rather than toward custom and formality, and a bias toward emotional fulfillment instead of duty or honor.

The rise of individualism is so important that it cannot be overemphasized. Since the late seventeenth century, the place of the individual has been dramatically altered. The individual has moved from being defined almost entirely by being a member of a family to attaining an independent identity. This has progressed so far that fostering individual identity is a major purpose of our marriages and families today.

The emphasis on personal affection in marriage has also increased because other roles that spouses formerly played in the family have now declined. Governments increasingly take responsibility for children's education, for the welfare of the elderly, and for the enforcement of laws in the community. As community involvement and solidarity have receded, individualism has increased. Affectionate relationships are increasingly emphasized in families because offering love and nurturance has been seen as the unique function of the family.

The emergence of individualism in the late seventeenth century can be seen in the growing attraction to introspection and to the individual personality. Increased attention to the individual also shows up at this time in the proliferation of personal portraiture, self-revelatory diaries, autobiographies, and love letters. This torrent of intensely personal artistic and literary forms signals an unprecedented interest in the inner self.[13]

The Enlightenment philosophers taught that the pursuit of individual happiness was the natural aim of human life. They justified their theories as natural law rather than seeking legitimacy in scripture. Individuals entered into contracts with spouses to enhance their happiness. These philosophers thought that they should not be compelled to enter into or remain parties to marriages that did not contribute to their individual well-being. These ideas helped transform marriage into a companionate relationship into which people entered freely, on the basis of mutual affection, in order to enhance their individual happiness.

A corollary to this emphasis on personal freedom and happiness was the humanist advocacy of divorce. Many philosophers portrayed divorce as a natural right and believed that making divorce more accessible would encourage spouses to treat each other better and improve their marriage. Their opponents countered that a good marriage was best secured through the difficulty of divorce. When spouses know that they were bound together for life, they would work out their disagreements, and they would make an effort to get along that they might not make if separation and divorce could be easily obtained. These two opinions have been reverberating through the last three hundred years. It is fascinating to recognize that in both perspectives divorce policy is a method of improving marriage. No one argued that divorce was good in and of itself until the late twentieth century. This persuasive emphasis on natural law and contract theory led inevitably to divorce's becoming more widely and easily available in almost all Western countries.

Two aspects of this development should be kept in mind, however. First, these changes were gradual and uneven, as social change generally is. The eighteenth-century call for personal freedom was extremely muted and remained tied to a strong conception of duty, whereas in contemporary America, we stress autonomy over obligation. Second, we usually see this increase in the range of personal freedom and self-expression as an unqualified good, but we must remember that it came at significant cost. Individuals lost a firm sense of their identity as part of an ongoing lineage, of themselves as links between past and future generations. There was also a decline in the availability of mutual support and assistance from the network of kin. The rise of the companionate marriage stripped away many of the external economic, social, and psychological supports for marriage and left marriages with little to hold them together except their emotional cohesion.

The Rise of Romance

By the early decades of the eighteenth century, the balance of decision-making power with respect to marriage had clearly shifted to the prospective spouses, but there was still universal agreement that sexual desire and romantic love were ruinous motives for marriage. By the middle of that century, however, the antiromantic viewpoint was fighting a losing battle against the rising tide of romantic novels and poems that heralded a new understanding of love and marriage. Public libraries in England made vast numbers of romances available, and women in particular read them avidly. Magazines published in postrevolutionary America had three times more references to romantic love than in the years preceding independence.[14]

It is impossible to say whether it was this literature that created romantic love, because they both arose together. It is clear that the popularity of romantic novels and romantic ideas about marriage marked a dramatic shift in English and American ideas about marriage, a shift that gradually spread to other Western countries.

For the first time in history, among the propertied classes in England and for everyone in America, romantic love became a respectable motive for marriage. Romance had always existed, of course, but the coupling of romance with marriage was quite new. As romantic love became more fashionable, it became more common. In a very real sense, a new form of sentiment had been created in the ideal of a lifelong romance with one's spouse.

In *The Family, Sex, and Marriage*, the historian Lawrence Stone recounts that in 1784 the Duc de La Rochefoucauld was charmed by the togetherness, harmony, and contentment he observed in English couples, by contrast with what he saw in French marriages. The companionate character of marriage also showed in the increasing warmth of the correspondence between spouses. Whereas spouses in earlier times had addressed each other as "Sir" or "Madam," they now began to use endearments and to make lengthy protestations of their love and of their unhappiness at being separated.

Stone relates an illuminating story about Richard Bignell, who was a clerk for an attorney named Alpin in the late eighteenth century. During his clerkship, Bignell fell in love with Alpin's daughter. At the end of his training, Bignell asked Alpin for his daughter's hand and was refused. When the father discovered that the two had been secretly married, he was incensed and disinherited his daughter. The townspeople of Banbury condemned the father's harshness, and many shifted their business from Alpin to Bignell.[15] Now, that's a romantic story!

The Exaltation of Romance and the Advent of Mass Divorce

The separation of the family from the outside world continued to deepen through the nineteenth century as romance and affection became ever more central to marriage. Alexis de Tocqueville's famous study *Democracy in America* describes the American home as private, and families as detached from society as a whole. The separation between the public and private realms was emphasized in two distinct value systems: independence, self-reliance, and ambition for the public realm, and love, mutuality, companionship, and self-sacrifice for the private domain. This separation was further emphasized as middle-class husbands were increasingly working outside the home and as their wives remained at home, occupied with domestic activities. This split between the home and the outside world was not complete, of course, for women were active in their churches, led reform movements, and provided numerous charitable services, which are clearly communal activities.

The gradual increase in the importance of personal feelings in marriage helps to show us that love, as an overriding factor in the quality and stability of marriage, is a very recent development. Even though the importance of mutual attraction in choosing a spouse increased, expectations for what we call *emotional fulfillment* had little to do with whether couples entered into marriage or terminated the union before the middle of the nineteenth century.[16]

Contrary to our modern assumption that marriages are made and maintained by love, spouses at this time did not necessarily expect their marriages to be emotionally gratifying so much as to enable them to have an orderly, virtuous life with a supportive companion and helpmate. In fact, there was remarkable agreement about the standards of acceptable marital conduct. Husbands were to provide the necessities of life, avoid polluting the home with excess drinking or gambling, and refrain from sexual excess with their wives. Women were expected to take care of household chores, bear and tend children, and remain chaste and modest in their behavior.

The Third Divorce Revolution

Rising expectations for marital companionship and harmony in the nineteenth century dramatically increased the chances of disappointment with marriage. This was particularly true because even as marital expectations increased, the social, ideological, and legal supports for marriage were becoming weaker. In England, Parliament decided to allow divorce proceedings in the courts for the first time in three hundred years because the volume of divorce cases had become overwhelming. Divorce was also transferred to the courts in places as diverse as New York, Sweden, and New Zealand.

In other countries, divorce laws were reenacted (France) or liberalized (Germany, the United States). This liberalization included expanding the grounds for divorce and making divorce less difficult and less costly. Many U.S. states made physical cruelty legal grounds for divorce. Under the pressure of plaintiffs and attorneys, judges gradually allowed the definition of cruelty to expand so as to include threats and acts of mental cruelty, such as constant nagging, humiliating language, and insults.[17]

Once again, as in a photographic negative, we see the changing definition of what marriage should be showing up in the acceptable grounds for ending the union. Adultery contradicts the ideal of sexual fidelity; abusive behavior is incompatible with affection and harmony; drunkenness undermines the ideal of moderation and sobriety needed for marriage. Thus the changes in divorce laws and practices were not designed to alter the conventional middle-class family but rather to reinforce its central features. The historian Elaine Tyler May argues that the grounds for divorce in Los Angeles in the 1880s "suggest that marriage was based on duties and sacrifices, not personal satisfaction. Spouses considered each other helpmates—providers and protectors of the home rather than partners in pleasure."[18] During these years, May argues, the increase in divorce resulted from the difficulty couples were having in living up to Victorian expectations. Spouses might disagree about whether they had breached these norms, but the standards themselves were never questioned.

May illustrates these standards with Lulu and Marcus Gilman, who had been married for eight years when Marcus, in 1873, filed for divorce on grounds of cruelty. He claimed that Lulu had neglected her domestic duties by going off to parties and amusements without him, unchaperoned. Because she appeared to be unchaste and was not fulfilling the duties expected of her, Marcus was granted the divorce.

There was an astonishing increase in the divorce rate in the second half of the nineteenth century. The divorce rate quadrupled in the United States between 1860 and 1910, and during the same period there were similar increases in England and Belgium. The divorce rate at the turn of the century was puny by modern standards, but at that time this dramatic increase was extraordinarily alarming. State legislatures enacted more than one hundred restrictive divorce laws, in an effort to reduce the divorce explosion. These new laws were an expression of anxiety about divorce, but they were futile. It became more difficult all across the United States to obtain a divorce, but the more restrictive laws were still unable to slow the increase in divorce.[19]

Romance and the Economy

The beginning of the twentieth century was marked by an acceleration in industrial growth. The maturing industrial economy began to produce unprecedented abundance, with higher wages allowing a tripling of consumer spending between 1909 and 1929. Commercial growth depended more and more on consumer spending, and the family increasingly became the engine of economic expansion.

The expectation of romantic love in marriage expanded dramatically around the beginning of the twentieth century. As love increasingly became the only valid basis for marriage, courtship grew to be more and more important. The quest for romantic love required women to devote themselves to their physical attractiveness and to cultivate the art of flirtation. Men had to acquire personality and charm. Dating and courtship became crucial activities for the young, and whole industries began to cater to the need to attract members of the opposite sex. The cultivation of romance is not cheap: it requires free time and money to finance entertainment, stylish clothing, and beauty aids. Between 1914 and 1925, revenues in the cosmetics industry increased from $17 million to $141 million.[20]

In the United States, the increase in consumer spending and the quest for excitement outside the home reflected a growing emphasis on personal happiness, and greater amounts of money and leisure gave rise to an expanded interest in entertainment. Joint participation in a moderate number of amusing leisure activities was one of the ways in which spouses expected to find happiness in marriage. For example, in the 1920s there was an increasing trend for a divorcing spouse to complain that his or her partner was either too involved in entertainment or insufficiently willing to seek amusement. Elaine Tyler May explains that people were torn between having an amusing spouse and a virtuous partner: "Women wanted their mates to be good providers as well as fun-loving pals; men desired wives who were exciting as well as virtuous."[21]

As material expectations continued to rise, husbands were expected to provide an increasingly higher standard of living. Between 1890 and 1920, economic considerations became much more prominent in divorce petitions. In a familiar pattern, material goods and conveniences that had been considered luxuries just a few decades earlier were now being transformed into ordinary necessities. One of the long-standing expectations for marriage was that husbands would provide adequate support for their wives. There was little disagreement about what was adequate in the 1880s, but by 1920 there was no clear standard for what was sufficient.

May refers, for example, to Norman Shinner's admission that he had deserted his wife after five years of marriage because he could not "support her in a manner she desired on my salary, and on this account we could not live together in an amiable manner."[22] Although Shinner earned an average living, he decided simply to leave rather than struggle to measure up to his wife's expectations.

Acceptance of Divorce

The debate over whether divorce was acceptable raged in the decades before and after the turn of the century, but as expectations for a happy marriage increased, the terms of the debate changed. By the end of World War I, the traditional idea that divorce was unacceptable had decisively lost. From then on, the debate centered on the contours of the new right to divorce. A new round of legal changes made divorce less difficult to obtain. In addition, divorce became noticeably less disgraceful during the 1920s. Divorce rates continued their gradual climb until World War II, after which there was a very high number of divorces until there came a leveling off in the 1950s.[23] It had become clear to most people that a return to patriarchal, indissoluble marriage was not possible. For this reason, and as a remedy for the alarming increase in divorce, experts on marriage seized on and further elaborated the idea of the romantic marriage. If spouses could learn to be affectionate and supportive, they would *want* to stay together. By the early 1930s, courses in marriage skills had begun to spread throughout the United States, on such topics as courtship, reproduction, and divorce. The advent of professional marriage counseling was another outgrowth of concern about the fragility of marriages. These efforts represented an important shift: couples would now be trained in the skills of maintaining a romance. This shift was described by Judge George Bartlett in the following way: "Mercy and justice to the mismated are creeping into the law. Divorce—like medical anesthesia—so lately despised, is beginning to be recognized as the next great step along the way. The way to where? The only answer is happiness."[24]

Beginning in the 1920s in America, sexual gratification in marriage began to take on an unprecedented role. Sex came to be seen as an expression of love, and a vigorous, harmonious sex life was touted as a cornerstone of a good marriage. This was no simple change, for the overwhelming tradition in the Western world had been to encourage sexual abstinence and restraint. This tradition focused on the chastity and purity of women. Men were to exercise restraint, in order to protect female purity, and men's measured involvement in sex, it was believed, would conserve their energy for more effective competition in the outside world.

By the 1950s, the ideal of the companionate family was dominant in the United States. Family togetherness was a watchword, divorce rates leveled off, and increases in income allowed the purchase of family homes. The popular media, psychologists, and educators emphasized that marriage was necessary to individual well-being. People who did not marry were characterized as immature, selfish, irresponsible, and deviant. Accordingly, the proportion of the population that married in America reached all-time highs.[25] Although America in the 1950s is often portrayed as the golden age of the family, that era was actually a very temporary respite from long-standing trends in the evolution of the family, such as increasing expectations for emotional fulfillment, growing tension between individual freedom and marital obligations, and increases in divorce.

The Triumph of the Individual

In the middle of the twentieth century, personal freedom became more important than ever before. As the widespread postwar economic expansion relieved financial concerns for the middle class, the quality of life became more closely related to having a rich emotional life. In what the authors of *The Inner American* call a "psychological revolution," Americans came increasingly to define happiness in psychological rather than situational terms.[26]

This cultural emphasis on psychological or emotional well-being meant that people now expected more psychological support and gratification from their lives. That expectation extended to marriage, which had come to be seen as one of the most important sources of personal well-being, as we saw in Chapter Two. But this raising of marital expectations led only to more frequent disappointment, and to even more divorces.

The aspiration to have a free, spontaneous, passionate love relationship is a very powerful ideal, one that in our society seems to define, at least in part, what a fuller or richer life is. Popular culture is awash in music, novels, and movies that glorify the emotional bond between partnered individuals. Dating services, personal ads, and meeting places provide abundant opportunities to connect with that special someone. All these aspects of popular culture express and perpetuate the idea that a gratifying romantic relationship is one of the most important aspects of life. The absence of this kind of relationship seems to imply that the quality or richness of one's life is crucially and irreparably diminished. In other words, involvement with another person in a mutually satisfying, intimate love relationship is generally seen as necessary if one is to live the full measure of the good life in the contemporary Western world.

It is ironic that some commentators have also portrayed the family as an impediment to individual self-development rather than as the deepest source of emotional fulfillment. We are torn between the aspiration for a deeply gratifying marriage that lasts a lifetime and the recognition that any relationship requires us to sacrifice some of our individual preferences. In the second half of the twentieth century, the demand for personal happiness became the central imperative in our lives, and we increasingly judge the adequacy of our marriages by whether they contribute to our happiness.

The dramatic increase in the social value of individual freedom and personal fulfillment, which reverberated through the 1960s and 1970s, was echoed by another dramatic acceleration in the divorce rate throughout the West. It is interesting to note, however, as the sociologist Barbara Defoe Whitehead does, that the doubling of the divorce rate between 1960 and 1980 was not accompanied by the kind of panic that the similar increase in divorce at the turn of the century had brought on. Divorce was no longer defined as a problem, because, according to Whitehead, divorce had become "expressive," by which she means that divorce was seen as a path to individual freedom and greater personal fulfillment.[27]

No-Fault Divorce: The Fourth Divorce Revolution

The advent of no-fault divorce constituted the fourth divorce revolution, and it truly was revolutionary because it dissolved the basic element of Western divorce: that a marriage could be terminated only when one of the spouses had committed an offense against marriage or against the other spouse. The central premise of no-fault divorce is that no grounds are necessary for divorce; all that is required is that one spouse assert the irremediable breakdown of the marriage.

The elimination of fault-based divorce is often blamed for the high divorce rate. Although no-fault laws may have contributed slightly to the acceleration in rates of divorce, increases in divorce were not generated by these laws because the dramatic increase in the divorce rate was well under way before no-fault laws were enacted.[28]

The enactment of no-fault laws makes a fascinating study in itself. Conservatives and liberals alike supported no-fault legislation. Conservatives hoped the law would help reduce divorce through family courts that were empowered to reject divorce petitions and to order counseling or education to salvage marriages. Liberals saw divorce as unavoidable, and they favored no-fault laws because such laws would make divorce less acrimonious and less destructive.

There was also a very strong drive to put an end to the legal charades that occurred in many divorces. Spouses frequently colluded to establish fictitious grounds for divorce, and this practice fostered perjury and hypocrisy while insulting the dignity of the court. Plaintiffs, attorneys, and judges had been stretching the legal grounds for divorce to such an extent that Herma Hill Kay, a leading figure in the no-fault movement, believed that nothing could make divorce easier in California than it already was. Very few divorce petitions were refused; 95 percent of divorce cases involved prefabricated stories that were told in ten-minute court hearings.

By the middle of the 1960s, divorce laws had been completely circumvented by division-minded spouses. The prevailing sentiment was that unhappy couples were entitled to divorce, and few judges were willing to place obstacles in their way. This pattern continued under the system of no-fault divorce as the family-court portion of the no-fault legislation was dropped, given the opposition to it from attorneys, judges, and legislatures. Surveys in California, Iowa, and Nebraska found that not a single divorce had been denied in thousands of cases brought before the courts in the 1970s. By 1980, all but two states had instituted no-fault divorce, and similar laws had been enacted in most European countries.[29]

No-fault laws were revolutionary in other ways as well. In many states, divorce is now available without the consent of one's spouse. Before no-fault divorce, the marriage contract had force, which meant that one had a "right" to remain married; now spouses have a "right" to be divorced. This change greatly facilitates divorce because it takes power away from the spouse who wants to stay married and shifts it to the spouse who wants to split up.

Once again, this change in divorce law reflects a shift in the prevailing expectations of marriage. Legislators, by eliminating the necessity of proving fault, decreed that spouses could decide, for any reason whatsoever, that their marriages were irremediable. Thus no-fault law marks the complete triumph of individual liberty in divorce regulation. Divorce has become an entirely personal decision. As the sociologist Lenore Weitzman puts it, "the new rules shifted the legal criteria for divorce—and thus for viable marriages—from fidelity to the traditional marital contract to individual standards of personal satisfaction. . . . The new divorce laws no longer assume that marriage is a lifelong partnership. Rather it is now seen as a union that is tenable only so long as it proves satisfying to both partners."[30]

Where Do We Go from Here?

There is no shortage of explanations for the gradual increase in the prevalence of divorce since the Protestant Reformation of the sixteenth century. For example, social scientists suggest that the explanation lies in such factors as the liberalization of divorce laws, changes in women's employment, and industrialization. In contrast, historians of marriage and divorce are virtually unanimous in rejecting the idea that these changes caused the evolution of marriage and the increase in divorce. Historians recognize that changes in divorce law and women's employment have helped provide the material conditions for changes in the divorce rate but have not caused people to end their marriages.

The central fact in the history of marriage is that over the course of the past four centuries our expectations for fulfillment in this relationship have risen enormously. We expect more from our marriages, and we have lower tolerance for unsatisfactory behavior and conditions. The popular author John Gray gives voice to the contemporary view of marriage in this way:

We demand and deserve lasting happiness, intimacy and passion with a single partner. If we don't get it, we are prepared to sacrifice the marriage; personal fulfillment is suddenly more important than the family unit. . . . Are we to turn back the clock and deny our own personal needs and suddenly make the family more important? In most cases, the solution is not divorce nor is it self-sacrifice. Instead, the answer lies in learning how to create relationships and marriages that support our personal fulfillment.[31]

This is the therapeutic vision of marriage that we will explore in the next chapter.

Lawrence Stone offers a historian's perspective on the modern family:

There is no reason to assume that the end-product of affective individualism, namely the intensely self-centered, inwardly turned, emotionally bonded, sexually liberated, child-oriented family type of the third quarter of the twentieth century, is any more permanent an institution than were the many family types which preceded it. . . . Nor is there any reason to assume that the family that has emerged in the late twentieth century must necessarily, in all respects, be more conducive to either personal happiness or the public good than the family types that have preceded it. Affective individualism is a theory which lacks any firm foundation in biological, anthropological or sociological data.[32]

This means that marriage's centrality to the good life is a social convention or agreement rather than a natural law of human behavior. It is relatively easy to understand, from a historical perspective, how we arrived at our current state of marriage, with all our confusion and dismay, but this does not mean that our difficulties were decreed by natural law. Marriage is a human institution that is shaped by human desires and imagination. The current form of marriage is a historical creation rather than a necessity. We can find a great deal of hope in the recognition that marriage was and is created by us, to fulfill our purposes. We are trapped in the contemporary paradox of marriage only when we fail to see that there are alternatives to our current understanding of marriage.

4

Marital Therapy, the Science of Marriage, and the Myth

In this culture, marriage may be the most popular
form of psychotherapy. We all seem to believe that
marriage will change our lives, will make us feel bet-
ter about ourselves. This is the magic union, the one
that has the power to transform reality.
        Augustus Y. Napier, The Fragile Bond[1]

Once we recognize that the myth of marital happiness creates such tremendous difficulties for us, we may well look to professionals, such as marital therapists or social scientists, for a less problematic alternative. We may hope that in the wisdom of the therapeutic community, or through the objectivity of science, we will obtain insights into getting beyond the myth. After all, we look to therapists for an objectivity that can help illuminate this kind of confusion, showing us how to be less self-defeating and more successful in such personal endeavors as marriage. We believe that science can help because one of its purposes is to liberate us from the thrall of myth and superstition.

Would it surprise you to learn that professionals, despite their diligence, intelligence, and specialized knowledge, are also caught up in the belief that the spouses' emotional fulfillment is the primary purpose of marriage, and that communication is the key to fulfilling that aim?

Marital Therapy

Let me begin by illustrating the power of this myth in marital therapy. There are a bewildering number of approaches to marital therapy, and we cannot talk about all of them here. We can learn a lot, however, by looking into two broad categories of marital therapy that are very widely practiced in various forms. The first focuses primarily on teaching communication skills as a way to help troubled couples. The second emphasizes the need to resolve the childhood wounds that create difficulties in marriage. Let's explore each of these popular approaches to marital therapy, to see if either can help us move beyond the myth of marital happiness.

Teaching Communication Skills

As we have seen throughout this book, communication is central to the conventional concept of a good marriage. Therefore, you won't be surprised that teaching communication skills is the single most widely used technique in marital therapy. Therapists believe that teaching communication skills helps spouses share themselves more fully, be good companions, experience intimacy together, and maintain or reinvigorate their loving feelings toward each other. Communication trainers tell us that good communication is also necessary to the solution of the many problems that arise in marriage.

What are the communication skills that so many therapists see as necessary to a good marriage? There are many variations in how therapists teach these skills, but most therapists emphasize skills in *listening* and *self-expression*. A brief description of these skills will help us better understand the therapeutic model of marriage.

Listening Skills

The first listening skill is *nondefensive listening,* or the ability to listen without becoming defensive. Listening nondefensively means focusing your attention on what your partner is saying and really attempting to understand what your partner means. When you listen nondefensively, you set aside the natural tendency to justify your-self, and you refrain from thinking or talking about why the prob-lem is your partner's fault. You can easily imagine how listening in this way can improve communication.

A second set of listening skills involves *active listening*. The sim-plest methods use what are called *minimal encouragers* (eye contact, nodding, saying "Mmm hmm"), actions that indicate your atten-tion and that encourage your partner to continue. Another skill in active listening is to paraphrase or summarize what your partner has said, to show that you have really listened and understood, or, if you have not, to give your partner the chance to clarify.

Yet another component of active listening involves validating your partner's statements. For example, you might say, "I can see how you would feel that way," or "I understand your perspective." Communication trainers emphasize that in validating one another, we are not necessarily expressing agreement. When you validate your spouse's perspective, you are only indicating that you can un-derstand why your partner sees the situation in a particular way. Val-idation is a way of saying that your partner's perception is legitimate, even if you do not agree with it. Validation can be very helpful be-cause one of the most destructive aspects of a heated argument is the tendency to communicate that your partner's perceptions are not valid.

Self-Expression Skills

Therapists also give training in *self-expression skills*, which help you communicate effectively and elicit less defensiveness from your part-ner. One of the most commonly taught techniques is the use of *"I" statements*, in which you state your perceptions or feelings as your own. This sounds simple, but it is rather difficult in practice. Train-ers teach couples to make statements like "I feel hurt when you don't answer my questions" rather than statements like "Why can't you an-swer a simple question? You are so rude!" You can easily see that each of these statements would probably engender a very different response. If you use "I" statements, you are much less likely to blame your spouse for a problem or a disagreement. "I" statements also convey that what you are saying is your subjective truth, and that it is also legitimate for your partner to see things in a different way.

A second self-expression skill is the ability to *ask your partner to change*. Communication trainers emphasize that these requests should be constructive and specific. They recommend that you focus more on the desirable positive behavior than on the negative behavior; doing so can help you avoid alienating your partner by emphasizing his or her flaws. In asking for change, you ask for what you want specifically, pinpointing the behaviors you want altered and the situations in which you would like the change to occur.

Communication trainers also teach partners skills in *problem solving* and *conflict resolution*. These skills usually take the form of such steps as defining the problem clearly, brainstorming solutions, choosing a solution, and so forth.

Benefits of Teaching Communication Skills

Helping couples become proficient in communication skills is at least as much education as it is therapy. Many professionals and clergy believe that teaching communication skills can help prevent marital distress before a couple becomes unhappy. I applaud this emphasis on prevention; as the old saying goes, a fence at the top of a cliff is far better than an ambulance at its foot.

There are many premarital preparation and marital enrichment programs that emphasize communication skills. For example, Diane Sollee has created an organization called the Coalition for Marriage, Family, and Couples Education, which hosts a large annual conference and lists more than forty national and international training programs for communication skills. A similar organization, the Association for Couples in Marital Enrichment, is dedicated to programs that are generally oriented to the improvement of couples' communication as a way to strengthen their marriages.

Skills trainers believe (and there is some research to support that belief) that teaching communication techniques increases spouses' feelings of intimacy, satisfaction, and harmony with each other and leads to better, more lasting marriages. The ability to communicate clearly and lovingly and the capacity to work out marital difficulties are wonderful things in a relationship.

Limitations of Teaching Communication Skills

Although the goals of teaching communication skills are good in many ways, they are also problematic. For one thing, it should give us pause to recognize that the goal of improving satisfaction through teaching communication skills is a major premise in the myth of marital happiness. What is more, the promotion of these teaching programs may further raise our already inflated expectations of marriage. Many trainers are very circumspect in how they describe their programs, but some authors actively intensify marital expectations, as you can see in the titles of their books: *Passionate Marriage, Hot Monogamy, 30 Days to a More Incredible Marriage, The Adventures of Intimacy, Communication Miracles for Couples, Being Happily Married Forever.*

Another problem with teaching communication skills is the questionable origin of these particular skills. Given the popularity of training in communication skills, it is important to consider how these skills were developed. For all the emphasis that skills trainers put on research, *the communication skills they teach are not scientific discoveries.* Therapists did not begin their search for communication skills by studying successful couples in order to learn how they communicated with one another and thereby discover the skills necessary to a good marriage. In fact, a recent study suggests that happily married couples, in their ordinary interactions, seldom use the communication skills touted by trainers.[2]

If the elements of these skills were not deduced through observation of successful couples, then where did they originate? The source of the communication skills favored by the trainers is their own training as therapists. There is a very high degree of overlap between the communication skills taught to novice therapists and the communication skills taught to couples. For example, therapists must learn to listen to their clients without letting their own emotions cloud their understanding (nondefensive listening). Novice therapists are taught how to encourage their clients to expand on and explore the difficulties with which they want help (active listening). A good therapist becomes a master of the ability to understand and communicate understanding of clients' perspectives and feelings, even when the therapist believes that clients may need a change of outlook (validation). Therapists in training are also taught to use "I" statements when they give feedback about the ways in which their clients' behavior is contributing to their clients' difficulties. Finally, therapists are taught to use role playing and educational techniques to teach new skills to clients. Making suggestions that highlight a client's strengths or telling a client how a particular skill will benefit him or her is parallel to the skill of requesting behavioral change from a spouse.

Although therapists' interviewing skills and couples' communication skills are not identical, the dramatic similarities are not at all coincidental: *therapists who teach couples communication skills are actually teaching spouses to be therapists to each other.* They are teaching couples a kind of professionalism and distance that is attained by listening without defensiveness or overt emotional expression, by validating someone even when you disagree, and by helping someone focus on what he or she can change that will make a difference. These communication skills require the ability to detach yourself, at least temporarily, from your emotions and from what is at stake in the conversation. According to trainers of communication skills, the best path to a better marriage is to become more like a therapist with your spouse. They say that doing this will help spouses feel better about each other and be happier in their marriage.

My wife and I have seen, at first hand, the overlap between training in therapy and training in communication skills. Susan and I met in a master's-degree training program in counseling. We went to classes together and worked in the same clinic. We became fast friends and spent a lot of time together before we realized that we were falling in love. When we began to see ourselves as a couple, we had to renegotiate our relationship.

Because we were both newly trained therapists, we naturally applied the communication skills we had learned to our developing relationship. When a problem or disagreement came up, we employed our communication skills and worked diligently on that difficulty. We would work and work and work until we had either ironed it out completely or completely exhausted ourselves. We would often be up half the night—communicating.

After a couple of months of this, we realized that our approach was just not sustainable: even if we could create the world's best relationship, we would never survive to enjoy it. So we began to ease up on the deployment of communication skills, relying more on our wonderful friendship to help us deal with problems. Through the years we have been together, our deep sense of being partners in life is what has been most helpful in creating the relationship that we both cherish so much. We do use communication skills to help, on occasion; but what keeps us going as a couple, more than anything else, is our joint commitment to ideals and goals that guide us in knowing how we want to live together.

Our aims in life are not especially complicated or unusual. We work to help each other pursue our callings in life, and we strive to raise our children so that they will become people of character and substance. We both sincerely want to build a shared life that embodies those goals. Most of our disagreements are small potatoes compared to what is really important to us, and once we remind ourselves of that, we are able to approach the little problems in a calmer and more cooperative way. In other words, communication skills are occasionally useful, but the real source of a strong marriage is the spouses' commitment to their partnership in life.

Marriage as Therapy

So far we have focused on a technique-oriented approach to marriage. Now let's turn our attention to therapists who emphasize a more self-expressive, personal growth-oriented form of marital therapy.

Healing Childhood Wounds

One of the most popular forms of growth-oriented marital therapy focuses on healing the childhood wounds that some therapists believe to be the source of marital difficulties. This is an idea that has emerged in many places and cannot be attributed to any one individual, but it has proved to be a compelling approach for many professionals and their clients.

Harville Hendrix, for example, has been enormously successful in popularizing this long-standing piece of marital therapists' shared wisdom. In his best-selling *Getting the Love You Want*,[3] he tells us that people seem to be attracted to the same kind of partners over and over again.

Hendrix calls his approach "Imago therapy" because he believes that we seek partners in the image of our early caretakers. He claims that we have detailed memories of the most minute characteristics of our caretakers, and that these memories form a "template" that creates both attraction to people who match it and an absence of romantic interest in people who do not.

Hendrix explains that this mechanism of attraction is not a matter of habit or blind compulsion. Rather, our romantic partnerships are part of our inherent urge to grow because they provide us with the opportunity to heal old childhood wounds. According to him, all of us were wounded as children. Our wounds range from slight misunderstandings and delays in caretaking to physical and sexual abuse. Even if you did not experience actual abuse, Hendrix claims, you along with everyone else were wounded by the message that certain feelings or behaviors were unacceptable to your caretakers, and that your parents only approved of you in part. Hendrix's Imago theory is that, because we feel a compelling unconscious need to heal these wounds, we choose partners who have shortcomings that are similar to the faults of our caretakers so that we can create a situation in which the healing can take place.

Imago therapists aim to transform the marital relationship into a therapeutic encounter in which each spouse fosters the other's psychological and spiritual self-completion. More specifically, the therapeutic procedures help the spouses reduce their defenses against intimacy, identify frustrations with the partner that grow out of painful childhood experience, and stop attempting to get their emotional needs met through behavior that is carried over from childhood situations. Imago therapists try to help spouses see each other realistically, develop compassion for each other, and help each other become whole. Much of the therapy is devoted to helping spouses learn to play an ongoing role in healing each other's childhood wounds. The idea is that the role of the therapist should become obsolete as each of the spouses becomes skilled in assisting the other's growth process.

In *The Family Therapy Networker*, a widely read professional magazine, Marian Sandmaier quotes Hendrix as saying, "The conscious marriage *is* therapy," and she goes on to say, "The core proposition of the Imago system is that people can and should get their childhood needs met through their partner—that, in fact, such healing is the deepest purpose and most glowing promise of the intimate relationship."[4] That is a remarkable statement: that the most important purpose of marriage is for spouses to provide therapy for each other. Think about it. These therapists are saying that the spouses' individual mental health should be the central preoccupation of the marriage, that "conscious" marriage has no higher purpose than the maintenance of the partners' fluctuating sense of psychological well-being. It is hard to imagine a more pronounced commitment to the idea that the purpose of marriage is to benefit the individual.

The Intensely Emotional Marriage

At the beginning of this chapter, I quoted Augustus Napier on "the magic union." In that quotation, he seems to be questioning the idea that marriage is a form of therapy, and he appears to be criticizing the popular-culture fantasy that a loving partner will make us feel strong instead of weak, whole rather than empty, comforted instead of lonely. He tells us that these high hopes are "modeled on the highly idealized 'good parent' images of early childhood" and that "the question is not whether this idealized relationship metaphor will fail, but when," and that when our disappointment surfaces, "all the rage and hurt of those early years may then pour out into our marriage."[5]

But Napier also believes that this experience is virtually inevitable because we are powerfully drawn to spouses who will help us reenact our early struggles with parents. He says that marriage is an unconscious experiment, one that not only recapitulates childhood struggles but also offers the possibility of transforming those dramas. Thus the primary themes of Hendrix's work are also central for Napier, a major figure in marriage and family circles.

Napier, in his very personal, engaging, and moving account of marriage, *The Fragile Bond,* tells us that the real issue in marriage is not whether we are always happy but how intensely we are involved with our partners. Good marriages, in his view, are characterized by the intensity of the emotional interchange between spouses—the degree to which partners can share sadness and anger with each other, as well as happiness.

Napier rejects the simplistic fantasy that marriage will make us feel strong, whole, and comforted. He makes it very clear that it takes a great deal of hard work and personal courage to reach the intimacy and mutual regard he identifies as the goals of marriage. He stresses that the emotional benefits of marriage do not come automatically, nor can marriage completely relieve the discomforts of the human condition. In his view, marriage cannot remove loneliness from life, because loneliness is part of being human, but developing an intense intimacy with a spouse can relieve the sense of being alone. Being married is not in itself enough to make us strong, but if we can work through childhood hurts with our partners, we can claim more of our personal power. Napier's understanding of the good marriage is certainly more realistic and nuanced than the popular dream. In the end, however, its shape is not all that different. Although Napier's is a more mature version of the myth of marital happiness, it is certainly a recognizable form of the myth.

Shall We All Become Therapists?

Isn't it fascinating that therapists and educators of widely different persuasions encourage us as spouses to become each other's therapist, either by obtaining therapeutic skills to enhance communication or by helping each other overcome childhood wounds? The communication skills touted by some therapists are to be employed in the service of marital intimacy and satisfaction. Similarly, those who promote the healing of childhood injuries through marriage extol this approach for its resultant personal growth and for the intimacy and fulfillment that this process brings to couples.

Therapists of all kinds warn against the "love conquers all" fantasy and offer a more realistic vision of the difficulties of marriage. But their insistence that we should employ therapeutic methods to enhance marital satisfaction and intimacy only emphasizes their commitment to marriage as a vehicle for personal emotional fulfillment. Clearly, seeing marriage as a form of therapy does nothing to take us beyond the myth of marital happiness.

These therapists have accepted the idea that there is no higher purpose in life than pursuing a more or less durable sense of personal well-being. They seem to believe that each of us is alone in a rather indifferent world, one that offers us the opportunity to decide for ourselves what we want from life as individuals. But this freedom also comes at the price of being thrown back on our own resources in order to understand life's inevitable suffering and difficulties. Indeed, in *The Triumph of the Therapeutic*,[6] Philip Rieff suggests that therapy emerged in the modern world as a way for isolated individuals to find fulfillment and come to terms with human sorrows, in the absence of a communal belief system that could provide answers to life's mysteries. Thus therapy is one avenue for obtaining the limited quantities of gratification that are available in a very imperfect world.

The marital therapists we have been discussing have accepted this bleak view of isolated individuals attempting to cope with a harsh, competitive world. They, along with much of Western culture, have adopted marriage as a primary vehicle of the quest for individual happiness and mental health. By making marriage therapeutic, they hope to encourage a "haven in a heartless world," to compensate for the missing connection between individuals and larger communal purposes and meaning.

If we accept that each of us is ultimately isolated, a completely independent individual, then marriage does seem like a way out of intolerable loneliness and despair. If we believe that our essential purpose in life is to feel happy, then therapeutic marriage provides an attractive path to that end. The problem is that our habit of seeing marriage primarily as a source of individual happiness has not worked out very well. Unfortunately, marital therapists have only added fuel to the fire of marital expectations with their well-intentioned efforts to make marriage more effective at providing individual satisfaction.

I do not want to be excessively critical of marital therapists. Many are in private practice, which means that they are in business. Remaining in business means that the products or services you offer must be those that consumers want. It is unreasonable to expect therapists to offer services that vary greatly from popular expectations. Moreover, therapists are socialized into the very same individualistic, personal fulfillment-oriented culture that gave rise to the myth of marital happiness. Marital therapy is a product of this culture and this time, and it is only natural that therapists, as participants in this way of life, should become proponents of the myth.

Moreover, offering a product that is attractive to consumers is particularly important for the most prominent spokespersons for marital education and therapy: those who offer workshops and publish in the popular press. The pressure to offer a simple method for attaining a happy marriage is very real in the mass market. I experienced this pressure at first hand. More than a dozen publishers declined to publish this book unless I wrote it as something like *Seven Simple Secrets You Use in Five Minutes a Day to Have the Marriage of Your Dreams*.

The Science of Marriage

If the pressures of the marketplace and the influence of culture have made it difficult for therapists to transcend the myth of marital happiness, then perhaps social scientists can offer a more objective viewpoint and shed some light on our dilemma. Let's look into whether research on marriage provides us with the kind of insights that can help us find a new direction for marriage.

We like to think of scientists as objective observers who begin from careful observation and gradually build theories that describe and explain various aspects of our world. Scientists want their theories to capture as much truth as possible about our world, and they work very hard to separate their personal and cultural viewpoints from their scientific work. Therefore, we might reasonably hope that social scientists would make important discoveries about the nature of a good marriage and about what makes it possible to have a good marriage. We might anticipate that an objective, scientific understanding of marriage would be distinct from the prevalent cultural ideals about marriage, in the same way that Copernicus's discoveries changed the ideas about stars and planets that were prevalent in his day.

Social Scientific Definitions of the Good Marriage

In their work, social science researchers use two broad concepts to identify good marriages. The first concept has to do with spouses' positive emotions about marriage (for example, marital satisfaction, adjustment, or happiness). I recently conducted a study of the terms that marital researchers use to describe marriage in their scientific reports. I found that *satisfaction* is by far the most commonly used term; in fact, it is used more than five times as often as any other term, whereas other words indicative of a good marriage, such as *commitment, loyalty, partnership,* and *teamwork,* are almost never used.

We might ask ourselves how social scientists decided that evidence of the spouses' positive feelings about their marriage was the best indicator of a good marriage. Did they go out and carefully study couples to discover the nature of a good marriage? No, they did not. From the very beginning of research on marriage, social scientists have simply *assumed* that personal experiences such as happiness, satisfaction, or adjustment define a good marriage. Thus the most common indicator that social scientists use to identify a good marriage comes directly from our cultural belief that happiness is the core of a good marriage. In this way, through the emphasis on feelings about marriage, the myth of marital happiness is built right into the very foundation of marital research.

What about the second way of measuring the quality of a marriage? Social scientists have also described a good marriage as stable, meaning that the couple is unlikely to divorce. Not surprisingly, researchers have found that they can predict divorce by finding out how many of the easily identifiable steps toward divorce a spouse has taken. First one or both spouses will contemplate divorce. One or both spouses will then begin to talk about it with others. This step is followed by actually planning a divorce, and finally by such concrete steps as seeing an attorney. The more steps either spouse has taken, the more likely it is that the marriage will end in divorce.

It is interesting to note that the stability of a marriage is somewhat independent of how satisfying the relationship is, which means that dissatisfaction with their marriage does not necessarily cause a couple to take steps toward divorce. In fact, many of us can recognize this combination of low satisfaction and high stability in our parents' and grandparents' marriages: fewer people today are willing to stay in a marriage that does not provide much satisfaction, but doing so was clearly a prevalent historical pattern. Many people view this pattern of marital stability with nostalgia, even if they would not choose it for themselves.

What, then, does marital research contribute to our concept of a good marriage? It tells us that satisfaction and stability are the key characteristics to look for in a good marriage. But the social scientists' choice to construe good marriages as satisfying and stable hardly strikes me as a robust picture of what marriage is all about. To say that satisfaction and stability make a "good" marriage would be like saying that a nation is "good" to the extent that its citizens have positive feelings about it and to the extent that the nation is not likely to undergo a civil war in the near future. But there is much more to a good nation, and to a good marriage. It is good to be happy in one's marriage, of course, and to feel that the marriage is stable, but isn't that a terribly meager description of such an important part of one's life?

We might forgive social scientists for failing to offer us a richer understanding of what makes a good marriage, for they believe that they should avoid questions of value (irony intended). They have used satisfaction and stability to assess the quality of a marriage because that is the prevailing cultural wisdom about what constitutes a good marriage. In this way, the researchers claim to be just describing what they have found, and perhaps we should not expect more of them by way of a definition of a good marriage. This means we may need to look elsewhere for a more robust understanding of what makes a marriage good, and in the second part of this book, we will do just that.

Social Scientific Explanations of the Good Marriage

What can social scientists tell us about why some marriages are more satisfying than others? Even though there are many theories, there are two basic explanations. One of them boils down to a simple notion: marriage is satisfying when it is rewarding (or at least more gratifying than the alternative). The other is based on the idea that good communication makes for a satisfying relationship.

Marriage as a Source of Rewards

The most widely used scientific theory of marriage is called *social exchange theory*, which tells us that a relationship is nothing more than a series of exchanges: we give our time and energy in various ways to our spouses, and we expect benefits in return. Social exchange theorists claim that spouses decide whether their marriage is satisfying by weighing the overall balance between costs and benefits in the relationship. They then compare that balance with what they believe the balance would be if they were in another relationship or were single. If the marriage stacks up well against the alternatives, then the spouses are likely to maintain it. If the marriage is less attractive than the alternatives, then, social exchange theorists believe, the spouses consider the barriers to ending their marriage. Barriers include such things as laws that make divorce difficult or costly, social disapproval of divorce, loss of property, and so on. If a relationship is less attractive than the alternatives, and the barriers to its ending are weak, then the couple is more likely to split up. This theory portrays spouses as hard-nosed comparison shoppers who restlessly evaluate whether they are getting the best relationship deal that the market can offer.

In a similar way, the *behavioral theory* of marriage tells us that rewarding interaction leads to marital satisfaction and stability, and that negative interaction undermines the quality and durability of the marriage. Behavioral theorists explain that spouses mutually shape each other's behavior through rewards and punishments. The more you do things that are pleasurable for your partner, the more your partner will reciprocate; partners also tend to respond in kind to negative or coercive behavior.

These two theories, and many others like them, tell us that our attachment to our spouses is primarily a bond of pleasure: we stay together because our marriage gratifies us. According to these social scientists, the most salient feature of a spouse is the degree to which he or she gives pleasure or causes pain. What is most interesting, however, is that even though social scientists value hard evidence above everything else, they present no evidence that spouses are fundamentally economic beings, or that emotional fulfillment is the primary aim of marriage. Instead of discovering the idea that plea- sure is central to marriage, they have assumed it from the beginning.

By presenting the social scientific theory that marriage is a vehi- cle for individual gratification, social exchange and behavioral the- orists give the stamp of scientific authority to the myth that marriage is all about personal benefit. If we accept these theories, then the myth of marital happiness is inescapable. These theories claim, in no uncertain terms, that spouses enter into a marriage for the rewards it provides and that they will leave the marriage if and when it be- comes insufficiently gratifying. For this reason, these theories actu- ally encourage individuals to operate primarily from self-interest and from concern with maximizing their personal fulfillment bottom line.

There is no doubt, of course, that humans are at least partly mo- tivated by pleasurable experience, and that contemporary marriage is one of the most important sources of good feeling. The real prob- lem lies in the fact that some professional researchers have pre- sented these theories as comprehensive descriptions of marriage, sufficient to encompass and explain all of marital and, indeed, human behavior. Far from providing an alternative to the myth of marital happiness, however, these social scientific theories rely on and even necessitate that myth.

Theories of Marital Communication

The second explanation for why some marriages are more satisfying than others is based on the idea that good communication makes for a satisfying relationship. Good communication may sound like a very reasonable, commonsense explanation for a good marriage, but we should ask why social scientists decided to study this particular aspect of marriage. Did they patiently, with no preconceptions, observe marriages and discover that stronger marriages had better communication? No. They began their research with the idea that communication is essential to a better marriage. They drew on our shared cultural vision of a good marriage: the myth of marital happiness.

Communication and marital happiness are inseparable in the conventional understanding of marriage. As we have seen, studies show that spouses do not distinguish their marital communication from their marital satisfaction. Spouses who report better communication virtually always tell us that they are happy in their marriages, whereas almost all those who tell us that they have poor communication also say that they are dissatisfied with their marriages. In other words, spouses are saying that a marriage is only good if it is characterized by good communication.

Social scientists take this overlap to mean that good communication brings about a good marriage. They do not recognize that the connection between good communication and satisfaction with marriage is derived from the myth of marital happiness. The dominant story of marriage today tells us that good communication is necessary to a good marriage; for most of our history, however, as we saw in Chapter Three, good communication and personal happiness have not been connected with a good marriage. There were other criteria for the goodness of a marriage: the proper performance of one's marital role, the begetting of an heir, and so forth. But, because we are convinced that feelings are the important thing, these historical ideals are not attractive to us.

The important point is that our definition of a good marriage has changed over time, and the way in which any society conceives of marriage is the result of social convention or agreement rather than the outcome of impersonal laws of nature. Thus, instead of discovering the truth about marriage, social scientists are simply documenting the myth of marital happiness. The problem, however, is that they are also mistakenly claiming to be uncovering the truth, and that by making such claims they are reinforcing the myth of marital happiness: the conviction that personal satisfaction is the only good available in marriage.

Even the very best research on communication and marriage accepts the conventional wisdom that communication is the key to a good marriage. John Gottman, one of the most widely known marital researchers, has conducted the most sophisticated research on communication in marriage.[7] He observes couples' communication, facial expressions, and physiological indicators of emotion in his laboratory. With the information he gains by these methods, he is able to make impressively accurate predictions of which couples will remain together and which will divorce. He also highlights other communicative behaviors—such as stonewalling, criticism, defensiveness, and expressions of contempt and disgust—as important predictors of low marital satisfaction and increased risk of divorce. He finds that when spouses treat each other badly, they become upset, feel less satisfied with their marriage, and are more likely to think about divorce, separate, and eventually divorce. Gottman realizes that this sequence is not particularly surprising, but he takes pride in being the first researcher to map the details of how it occurs.

It is no wonder that Gottman has received so much attention for his work. The precision, systematic character, and predictive success of his research bring it much closer to an ideal that is seldom attained in social science. And yet I wonder how much we have really learned from all this careful work. Starting with a simple notion—that poor communication leads to marital dissatisfaction and divorce—Gottman has clearly taken it to a new level of specificity and precision. It has now been scientifically confirmed that spouses who ignore, nag, criticize, or show contempt for each other are more likely than other couples to divorce. Yet how surprising is that? For all its valuable scientific underpinnings, such a discovery does not take us very far from the common wisdom about marriage.

Individualism, the Myth of Marital Happiness, and Marital Research

> It is not likely that the domestic domain will ever be
> able to satisfy completely the great expectations for
> individual fulfillment brought to it. As long as the
> American pursuit of happiness continues along this
> private path, divorce is likely to be with us.
> Elaine Tyler May, Great Expectations[8]

It is clear that there is a great deal of overlap between research on marriage and the common wisdom about it. Are social scientists simply discovering that the common wisdom about marriage generally reflects the truth?

I think there is a much better explanation for the consistency between scientific and popular ideas about marriage—namely, that the science of marriage is completely caught up in the contemporary cultural understanding of marriage as a source of emotional gratification for the partners. The intermingling of contemporary popular culture with social science shows up unmistakably in researchers' emphasis on the spouses' satisfaction with marriage and in researchers' seeing communication and pleasure as the keys to a happy marriage.

Professionals, rather than discovering and describing ultimate truths about marriage, are captivated by contemporary, conventional ideals of marriage. This is obvious if we simply recall the many different forms marriage has had in our history, many of which have had nothing to do with communication skills or satisfaction. The high degree of overlap between the popular and professional views of marriage makes it clear that social science has not helped us transcend the myth.

The core of most social scientific theories is the *assumption* that individuals are autonomous beings who have appetites and desires that they try to gratify as much as possible by using the most effective strategies available. Scientists usually see relationships, marriage included, as contracts or arrangements through which individuals satisfy their needs and desires. Scientists did not *discover* that spouses are independent individuals who seek emotional fulfillment in their marriages. There is no careful, well-documented research that establishes this key premise; social scientists have assumed it from the beginning. These assumptions about individuals and their relationships reflect the central premises of individualism, the dominant philosophy of contemporary American life, which helped inspire the myth of marital happiness.

Some social scientists will cry "foul" at this assertion. They may say it is not their place to question or criticize social mores or values, and that they are only attempting to describe and explain the social world as it is. Marriage and divorce do take place on the basis of whether relationships are satisfactory, researchers say, and they only attempt to map this reality. They profess neutrality about what they study, actively eschewing any position on such things as the value of marital satisfaction. They believe their job is to work within the given social realities and let people make their own decisions about values.

But this scientific disclaimer misses the point because the myth of marital happiness is at the heart of the confusion and problems we are currently experiencing with marriage. Social scientists not only fail to question this myth but also endorse it by conducting research that assumes the centrality of the individual and sees marriage primarily as a source of individual benefit. This endorsement is very powerful because researchers place the prestige and authority of science behind the idea that marriage is really about emotional fulfillment. To the extent that the science of marriage adopts an individualistic understanding of marriage and accepts the myth of marital happiness as a reality, marital scientists convey the idea that the myth actually *is* the ultimate reality.

If I am correct, then social scientific research on marriage cannot help us resolve the marital difficulties that grow out of this myth. The confusion of marital convention with marital truths may explain why decades of marital research, even though a great deal of it has had the explicit or implicit goal of reducing the divorce rate, has not really helped us reverse the appalling trend of divorce in our society. Moreover, the scientific emphasis on studying and improving marital satisfaction, intimacy, and communication may actually be increasing pressure on the marital relationship, for these efforts further inflate popular expectations that are already excessive. The unfortunate entrapment of the science of marriage within the ambit of the myth of marital happiness means that standard social science cannot help us circumvent the paradox of marriage.

If neither marital research nor marital therapy can take us beyond the myth of marital happiness, then what alternative, if any, do we have to this self-defeating myth? There are hints about a deeper vision of marriage in the literature on marital therapy and marital education. As we have seen, marital therapists make it clear that the joys of a satisfying marriage require sustained effort on the part of spouses.

Hidden within this relationship "work ethic," and within the emphasis on the therapeutic role that professionals have outlined for spouses, we find a central component of a good marriage: *virtue*. As we will see in the next chapter, employing communication skills and helping your partner overcome childhood injuries requires you to possess significant character strengths. Therapists do not discuss these virtues directly, but they are always just under the surface. It is important for us to give marital virtue more attention: learning how to act virtuously in marriage can take us beyond merely *feeling* good in marriage and show us the way to *being* good in marriage.

Part II

A New Vision
of Marriage

5

Creating the Good Marriage
From Technique to Character

Goodness is the only investment that never fails.
Henry David Thoreau[1]

We have now seen that there is an overwhelming consensus among the general population, therapists, and researchers that communication is the key to a good marriage. As we all know, communication can be difficult at times, and many experts recommend that couples learn communication skills as a way of bolstering their ability to maintain their love and work out their differences. I was trained in these skills myself and have taught them to many couples. I began to see the flaws in this approach when I noticed that some spouses had learned the skills and were able to use them in practice sessions with me but could not apply the skills with their partners.

One couple I worked with a few years ago, Sandy and Ben, helped me recognize this weakness in the skills approach. They had been married for fourteen years, and both spouses had successful careers and social lives. Ben managed a substantial department of city government in a medium-size city, and Sandy was the executive director of a small but well-respected medical clinic that offered services to the poor. They came to see me because they were embroiled in a long series of running arguments that had become progressively more aggressive and destructive.

At the time they came to see me, Ben reported that they were having at least one major argument every week and that these arguments were teetering on the verge of physical violence. As happens with most couples, the disputes would often start out with some minor detail of daily life but would quickly escalate to the point where Ben and Sandy were saying everything they could to hurt and humiliate each other. After twelve years of marriage, they knew each other's weak spots with great precision. Once they were angry, they would batter away at each other verbally, without mercy. The situation had become intolerable.

We worked together to identify some of the triggers for their anger, and we began to tie the seemingly minor issues to the things that really got under their skin. For example, Sandy thought Ben spent too much money frivolously, without consulting her. Ben felt that Sandy frequently treated him like a child and that in arguments she used her greater verbal skill to tie him up in knots. What is more, both admitted doing these and other things at times, because each knew these things bothered the other.

As this picture became clearer, we worked on interrupting their escalating arguments by identifying the points at which they could still decide to stop. Sandy and Ben, like many other people, often felt that events carried them away and that they could not control their actions. With some effort, they both gained the ability to pinpoint the signs that they were about to become verbally abusive. Learning to recognize the point of no return for their anger could also allow them to interrupt an argument before it became ugly. That was the theory, at any rate.

I began to teach them communication skills, and both of them were very quick to understand the skills and recognize how they could be applied. We practiced the skills in our sessions. At first, to make the practice easier, Ben and Sandy each practiced role playing only with me. Then I began having them practice with each other in session. Sandy and Ben demonstrated that they could use the skills in both formats. They were a little skeptical about whether the skills would work for them, but many couples express these doubts before successfully using communication skills. Both agreed to try to interrupt their arguments at home before they spiraled out of control, and to use their newly acquired skills to resolve issues rather than attack each other.

For several weeks, we continued to practice the communication skills, discuss the arguments they had at home, and improve their ability to communicate. This was grueling work for all of us because their arguments were very passionate, and it was very difficult for them to maintain their focus on working out their conflicts, even when I helped them in our sessions. Our success with this approach was very limited.

Ben and Sandy were becoming discouraged about their prospects for changing their marriage, and I felt that we should step back and take stock of what we were doing. I asked them what kept them from exercising at home the skills we had practiced in our sessions. Ben said, "It all makes so much sense when we discuss how to talk to each other in here. I really want to do better, but when Sandy starts in on me, I get so angry that all I want to do is hurt her back. I'm not proud of that, but when she gets under my skin, I just forget about working out the fight, and I just go after her." As we explored this issue, Sandy admitted that she was frequently less interested in solving the problem at hand than in making Ben feel small and trying to force him to admit he was wrong.

Ben and Sandy had shown me, however, that they were able to use the communication skills in relatively calm periods during our sessions. They genuinely wanted to improve their marriage. Yet all our painstaking work on these skills—including the skill of stopping the fight before it got out of hand—would go out the window as soon as they got home and became angry with each other.

What I saw with Ben and Sandy is something I have seen with many other couples since: teaching them communication skills was simply not enough; they could not use the skills because they could not or would not rein in their anger. They both felt that striking out at the other was necessary and that restraining their anger was not an option when they were fighting.

Communication and Virtue

The kind of self-restraint necessary to stop the cycle of attack and defense in which Ben and Sandy were caught was not available to them. But self-restraint is not really a skill; it is more a personal strength, or an indicator of character—in short, a virtue. Exercising appropriate control over our impulses and emotions is something we must do frequently in our interactions with others. In fact, one thing that helped Ben and Sandy learn greater self-control was their realization that they already were exercising a degree of self-restraint. Ben wanted very much to hit Sandy when she talked circles around him and left him feeling like a foolish child, but he did not hit her. Sandy recounted her persistent impulse to destroy some of Ben's prized stereo equipment when she was frustrated with him, but she did not do it.

The complete ineffectiveness of communication skills in the absence of self-restraint made it clear to me that something important had been omitted from the approach that uses skills training: self-restraint is essential to the use of communication skills. Marital researchers and therapists present communication skills as one of the answers to marital distress, but they do not recognize that virtues such as self-restraint are necessary for using these skills. Although researchers and therapists do not acknowledge that virtues are inherent in the use of communication skills, their emphasis on practicing these skills and working on your marriage points the way to recognizing the role of virtue in marriage.

Nondefensive Listening and Self-Restraint

The most sensible place to begin our exploration of the connection between communication skills and virtue is with the first, most basic communication skill: nondefensive listening. This skill is important because it is the foundation for many of the other key communication techniques.

You will recall that listening nondefensively means focusing your attention on what your partner is saying rather than defending yourself or blaming your spouse. This is obviously very difficult to do in a conflict—just when communication skills are especially important—because one of the first things spouses do when they disagree is to blame each other and defend themselves. This pattern of blaming our partners and defending ourselves can perpetuate itself indefinitely, as we saw with Ben and Sandy, because defending ourselves seems to be the sensible thing to do when we feel attacked, and blaming our partners is one of the strongest ways to defend ourselves.

Nondefensive listening seems to be a very sensible way to combat this destructive pattern, and teaching this skill can be very helpful. Unfortunately, however, every marital therapist will tell you that there are many individuals, like Sandy and Ben, who simply cannot or will not learn to use this skill. These individuals seem unable to restrain their impulses toward self-defense long enough to listen to and really hear what their partners have to say. When partners do not practice the necessary self-restraint, their unfettered emotional volatility makes it impossible for them to apply their communication skills, even if they have learned the techniques perfectly.

Nondefensive listening requires a lot of self-restraint, particularly when we disagree with our spouses about something important and when our passions run high. Restraining the impulse to dispute our partners' perceptions and justify ourselves is far from easy in this circumstance.

The ability to use this central communication skill often depends on our capacity to prevent ourselves from doing or saying what comes naturally to us. Nondefensive listening requires us to rein in our impulses and marshal our energies to *work on* our relationships. We can see that self-restraint is a virtue because it requires us to resist acting on our impulses of the moment in order to pursue a higher goal: a harmonious relationship. As we will see later, the practice of virtue is not just grim self-control; rather, we learn to act virtuously because we can recognize what is best and because we want to act in ways that bring about the best.

You are probably wondering how Ben and Sandy's marriage turned out. They were able to develop a much better marriage, partly because they both possessed the virtue of loyalty, which we will examine in depth in Chapter Seven. Because they were loyal to each other, they were willing to stick it out and endure some very difficult times in order to create a better marriage. The key to their improvement, however, was our recognition that they lacked self-restraint in their interactions. We talked about what made it so hard for them to hold back their vicious assaults on each other. They both talked about how their interactions had become one long series of one-upmanship and revenge. Each of them was preoccupied with getting the best of the other.

As we talked, they both realized that neither of them had ever had anything like a complete or sufficient victory. Even when it seemed as if one of them had decisively won a battle, the other would soon turn the tables. As they recognized the futility of their efforts to win, they became willing to rein in their destructive impulses. There was a great deal of work left for them to do, and they had to learn to trust each other and forgive each other for the myriad hurts that they had inflicted. But their recognition that they could choose either self-restraint, endless warring, or divorce helped them rebuild their marriage.

Active Listening, Self-Restraint, and Generosity

When you use active listening, as we saw in Chapter Four, you encourage your spouse to talk: you make eye contact, nod, and paraphrase what your partner has said. Doing these things helps ensure that you are listening, and when you restate what your partner has said, you allow him or her to correct any misunderstandings. The skill of active listening, as we have seen, also involves validating your partner's statements.

You will already have guessed the skill of active listening depends on self-restraint, for the same reasons that nondefensive listening does. To be able to listen, you have to restrain your desire to talk. You have to direct your attention to what your partner is saying. It takes even more self-control to encourage your partner to go on and say more when your partner is upset with you. Going beyond nondefensive listening and encouraging your partner's self-expression during an argument often requires you to contain powerful personal reactions.

Active listening goes beyond self-restraint, however. Encouraging your partner to speak is also an act of generosity because it is a gift of your attention and interest: when you listen attentively, you are granting that your spouse has something worthwhile to say. Spouses can be generous or miserly with their attention to each other. Making gestures that prompt your partner to speak is only meaningful when you are willing to give your attention. I am using the term *generosity* in a more expanded sense than Aristotle and other premoderns would have employed. Whereas they understood generosity primarily in terms of being openhanded with money, generosity in its modern usage means the willingness to give or share talent, goods, money, or oneself. The modern definition is clearly more broadly applicable to a relationship like marriage.

The skill of validation—that is, acknowledging the validity of your partner's point of view—can demand an even greater degree of generosity. Granting the legitimacy of your partner's point of view is a precious gift at any time. Communicating that you think your partner's opinion is valid is a powerful kind of support and understanding, one that the ungenerous seldom offer. Validation can only be given, never forced, if it is to have any meaning or effect. Seeing your spouse's perspective as valid requires still more generosity when your partner has an opinion different from yours, even when there is no real conflict involved. It involves giving your partner the benefit of the doubt.

Validating your partner's viewpoint in the course of a disagreement can be very difficult because it is so hard to acknowledge that someone has a valid point of view when we disagree with him or her. This is particularly true when the dispute is about personal matters in a marriage. Validation can be excruciating when your partner is questioning your responsibility, competence, consideration, or caring in the relationship. Being able to validate your partner's point of view when it is unflattering to you in this way involves an almost heroic level of generosity. Giving your partner credit for rationality and good intentions, for all the usefulness of this act, can be extremely taxing during a marital disagreement.

The spouses in a troubled marriage characteristically refuse to credit each other with rationality and a legitimate point of view. In such a marriage, the partners often insist on interpreting each other in the most negative possible terms. This lack of generosity leaves very little room for good communication, and it goes a long way in perpetuating marital conflict.

The cultivation of this kind of generosity was important for Dan and Felicia, who came to see me because their communication had broken down. Dan, a stolid Midwesterner, had fallen hopelessly in love with Felicia, a first-generation Cuban American woman, five years before. They married a year later, still very much in love, but found themselves arguing almost daily.

One of the most frequent and intense conflicts was related to the remodeling of their home. Dan worked long hours in his law firm, and Felicia was a full-time homemaker. She had taken over the day-to-day management of the remodeling because she was available. Dan was frequently upset because Felicia did not consult him about remodeling decisions. He accused her of usurping control and of lacking interest in his wishes. Felicia countered that it was frequently very difficult to find Dan when a quick decision was necessary. She added that when they did talk about how to proceed with the remodeling, Dan always delayed the work by worrying about the details or by wanting to investigate other options. She felt that consulting him meant only delay and that if he could have his way, they would never finish the work. As the homemaker,

Felicia bore the brunt of the remodeling and of the disruptions that the work caused in their schedule.

I assisted Dan and Felicia in working through this impasse by helping each of them see the legitimacy of the other's point of view. Dan was gradually able to appreciate that Felicia's primary goals were to have a comfortable home for themselves and their children and to be finished with the overwhelming mess that the remodeling created. He began to recognize how his unavailability and cautious nature made it seem impossible for his wife to seek his input. Felicia was able to reinterpret Dan's slower pace as caution and as a desire to refashion the house so that they would be happy with it for many years. She found a way to believe him when he told her that he was doing his utmost to be available to her rather than avoiding her when she called or paged him.

Felicia and Dan were gradually able to reclaim their love and partnership by progressively extending trust to each other and giving each other the benefit of the doubt instead of seeing each other's actions in a negative light. The generosity they cultivated also helped them see each other in a more positive light and allowed each of them to recognize the other's good intentions. Because generosity is so important to a good marriage, we will explore it in greater detail in Chapter Eight.

Self-Disclosure, Honesty, and Courage

As we saw in Chapter Four, communication trainers recommend a set of skills for self-expression in marriage, in addition to the listening skills we have been discussing. These skills include the use of "I" statements and the practice of asking for specific changes in your partner.

It is easy to see that we must possess at least two more virtues to make significant self-disclosure possible. One is honesty, or truthfulness. The other is courage.

Honesty is clearly necessary in self-disclosure, which is nothing but a sham if we do not share our thoughts and feelings truthfully.

This may seem so plain as to be hardly worth mentioning, but it is just this obviousness that has made it easy to overlook honesty as a necessary virtue in communication training. Professionals seldom mention truthfulness in their descriptions of the communication training they do. When they do mention it, they almost never refer to it as a virtue. They simply assume that people are being honest when they express themselves to their partners.

Revealing important aspects of ourselves often has the pleasant result of drawing us closer to our partners, but enhanced intimacy is not guaranteed. Expressing our feelings and asking for change may also require us to engage in significant self-disclosure, which exposes our feelings and desires. It is often much safer to criticize our partners or remain silent, because when we reveal what we want or what bothers us, we leave ourselves open to being disappointed and hurt.

Our fear of this vulnerability is one of the reasons we are reluctant to share ourselves fully with anyone else, even our spouses. But when we choose to do something in spite of our fear, we are acting courageously. Making ourselves vulnerable by telling our spouses how we feel or by asking for what we want in the relationship requires courage. Once again, I am using the term *courage* in a broader way than Aristotle would have used it. My usage is consistent with the general concept of courage, but it is a significantly less extreme concept than the battlefield-variety courage to which Aristotle typically referred (even though some couples' interactions resemble nothing so much as a battlefield).

Our understandable fear of vulnerability means that we generally disclose our feelings gradually, and that our self-expression becomes deeper only with time, and as trust develops. Nevertheless, each new revelation involves risk, and each new risk requires courage to undertake. This is even more true when a couple is experiencing significant conflict, characterized as it often is by misunderstanding and hostility. Yet communication trainers recommend significant self-disclosure during conflict: letting our partners know what upsets us, expressing our feelings, and asking for specific changes. No wonder our courage fails us at times, given the rigors and vulnerabilities in-volved in this kind of communication!

Editing, Self-Restraint, and Judgment

When communication trainers encourage self-disclosure, they wisely caution couples not to use honesty as an excuse for striking out de-structively. For this reason, they suggest another skill called editing. In calmer moments, it is obvious that we need to decide carefully what to say to our partners and how to say it. It is sometimes sur-prising how frequently we neglect to edit our communication with our partners, especially when we are upset. We can only carry out the common-sense suggestion to edit what we say to our partner if we can exercise self-restraint. Editing is, first of all, refraining from saying things we might like to say because they are destructive.

Another capacity we must possess if we are to edit our commu-nication effectively is judgment. This kind of judgment has noth-ing to do with criticizing other people; rather, it is the capacity to recognize what is important in a particular situation, and which ac-tions are best, given that situation—the ability to differentiate be-tween what will be appropriate or helpful in the circumstances and what will be harmful. As we will see, judgment is a key to virtue. Let us now explore the concept of virtue, before fully discussing the importance of judgment.

What Is Virtue?

It is from a man's choice that we judge his character.
Aristotle[2]

I first became aware that virtue is a necessary component of com-munication skills when I realized that virtues such as self-restraint, courage, and honesty are essential to the use of these skills. As I have observed and spoken with many couples, I have recognized that there are many virtues that can contribute to a good marriage.

I want to explore four virtues in depth in Chapters Six through Nine: friendship, loyalty, generosity, and justice. I call them *partnership* virtues, because practicing these virtues not only facilitates good communication but also helps us create the best kind of marriages: relationships that are lifelong partnerships. Of course, there are other virtues that can be helpful and other ways to characterize these virtues, but I chose to describe these virtues because they can contribute so much to a vibrant marriage. Before examining the partnership virtues in detail, however, let's take some time to clarify what I mean by *virtue*.

We have many associations to virtue, some positive and some negative. As a reaction to our Victorian past, we sometimes adopt a prejudiced view of virtue that leads us to see it in negative terms. In many of our stories, virtue is often depicted as priggishness: a character who takes himself to be virtuous is merely self-righteous or small-minded. Other portrayals present virtue as a pointless kind of self-denial whereby someone, in the service of a misguided aloofness or sense of superiority, refuses to enjoy life. Another strategy that has been used to discredit virtue is the revelation of hypocrisy behind virtue's façade. There have been many instances of all of these failings, of course, but there is no reason for us to be so jaundiced and prejudiced as to believe that no one can sincerely and fruitfully practice virtue. For example, every day I see people around me acting virtuously, without pretense or ostentation.

There are many good portrayals of virtue, but I have chosen to focus on Aristotle's account because I find it particularly illuminating. (I am especially indebted to Sarah Broadie's fine study *Ethics with Aristotle*.[3]) In Aristotle's portrayal of virtue, there is no place for self-righteousness, superiority, hypocrisy, or aloofness. He maintains that virtuous acts are not ends in themselves—things we do just because we should; rather, he teaches that the good person acts virtuously to foster human flourishing, by which he means living the best sort of life through fulfilling our highest nature. More than in words or attitudes, virtue shows up in *actions* designed to bring about the good. For example, we can recognize courage in a person by how she acts to master her fear so that she can do what she must to accomplish a worthwhile goal. This means that virtuous acts, for Aristotle, are our efforts to bring out the very best in ourselves and in our society.[4]

This relationship between our actions and the ideals and purposes we espouse in our lives is central to virtue. Indeed, *we act virtuously when we engage in some action for the sake of a higher good*. For example, if you exercise self-restraint in your communication, you are giving up the gratification of less worthy impulses, such as seeking revenge or power, in favor of something more worthwhile: the cultivation of a good marriage. Thus, communication trainers encourage spouses to restrain their defensiveness and rebuttals, not out of a long-suffering martyrdom but for the sake of an important goal: a better marriage.

Virtue and the Good

Aristotle defines virtues as those character traits that make it possible to flourish as a human being, to be fully human. His writings on ethics are notorious for leaving the definition of human flourishing ambiguous. At times he seems to say that the highest form of human activity is the creation of the best possible communal life, and yet he seems to conclude his *Nichomachean Ethics*[5] with the claim that contemplation is the highest good of humans because, in using our minds, we realize what is most distinctive about being human and come closest to the divine.

Aristotle seems to be convinced that he can really identify the ultimate good for all human beings. Because we value pluralism, it seems enormously arrogant to us for anyone to claim to know what is right or good for everyone. I certainly do not believe that I know what is the best kind of life for everyone, and yet I do think that in any society there is a limited number of reasonable alternatives for a good life, and we choose our way of life from among the alternatives open to us. Moreover, we always live out some understanding of what is worthwhile in life because our choices and actions are very powerful statements about how we think we should live. (In Chapter Six, we will explore a number of different ways in which couples define the good life for themselves.)

Virtue in Action

Aristotle emphasizes that virtues must be seen in action. He describes virtue as a well-established disposition to act for the sake of the good. There are intellectual and emotional aspects of virtue, but there is no such thing as a virtuous thought or feeling that does not relate to a virtuous act. For example, you probably would not credit someone with courage if she had brave thoughts but did not carry those thoughts into action. The intellectual aspect of virtue is important because acting virtuously requires an understanding of the virtue and when it is appropriate. Simply throwing yourself into a dangerous situation is not so much an act of courage as of foolhardiness—an impulsive defiance of danger rather than a reasoned act that fits the circumstance.

When we embrace a set of ideals as defining what is truly good in our lives, we decide that some activities are more important to us than others. We are more likely to do the things that are associated with what we think is worthwhile in life. By choosing a set of ideals, we also open ourselves to being swayed by certain reasons for acting in one way rather than in another. In other words, because we have adopted certain ideals, we choose to act in particular ways for the sake of those ideals. For example, a person who has adopted the idea that the most important thing in life is to acquire money and material goods will be inclined to see and pursue opportunities for these acquisitions. Credible invitations to increase his holdings will be persuasive, as will inducements to work long hours and engage in practices that increase his profits, even if doing so is costly to others.

Success in pursuing the aims that we have adopted for our lives requires development of the personal characteristics necessary to such pursuit. Success in maximizing acquisitions, for example, depends on the ability to recognize fruitful opportunities, the courage to take risks, persistence in the face of adversity, and a willingness to work very hard, among other traits.

It is the same in the realm of marriage. The contemporary ideal of a satisfying marriage requires the ability to communicate well, which in turn calls for the development of such traits as self-restraint and the cultivation of courage, among other virtues.

Cultivating Virtue

Aristotle reminds us that virtues do not necessarily come naturally to us and must be cultivated. But if virtues are not natural to us, neither are they contrary to our nature. Virtues are acquired characteristics because virtuous action frequently differs from acting on our first impulse. Thus learning virtue means cultivating our feelings so that they, too, are consistent with virtuous activity.

We all have the potential to act virtuously but can do so only with proper guidance and practice. Cultivation is an apt metaphor for the development of virtue: the best fruits, vegetables, and grains come from strains of plants that have been carefully developed over a long period and that require special treatment to come to fruition. These food crops were developed from plants found in nature, but they only attained their current value and taste through hundreds of years of horticultural effort. Virtues can take root in our lives if we foster them with appropriate care and attention; that is, we take what is natural in us (our thoughts, our feelings, our actions) and shape it in order to become the best people we can be.

We learn how to be virtuous by receiving guidance and encouragement from others who know more about virtue. Much of this learning on our part takes place in childhood, when we are taught basic lessons about good character. If we are open to virtue, we can continue to learn about it throughout our lives from inspiring stories or from teachers, ministers, rabbis, therapists, friends, and family members. Sometimes we are taught through words, but often we learn by watching others act virtuously. Instruction and example can take us only so far. The exercise of virtue is an activity: to be virtuous, we must act virtuously. Having character means acting in a way that is habitually virtuous, and we develop good habits through virtuous action.

This process is a lot like the way we learn manners or skills. It requires guidance and practice. For example, we learn what it means to be courageous from others who act courageously, and then we learn to be courageous ourselves by practicing courage. We actually make ourselves into people of good character by practicing virtue. Our actions shape us, and by choosing to act well, we reinforce our tendency to do so, and we encourage our virtuous feelings. As we develop the habit of virtue, it becomes easier and easier to act well. This is the behavioral aspect of developing virtue: we shape ourselves to virtuous habits by consistently acting virtuously. The goal is for virtue to become second nature to us—for it to come naturally.

Aristotle emphasizes that virtuous action also involves intellect and feelings. Virtuous action depends not just on what we do but also on doing the right thing for the right reasons, and knowing that we are acting for the right reasons. In a conversation, for example, a spouse might appear to be exercising self-restraint by refraining from interrupting, but his silence might actually be a result of his being afraid to talk, or of his thinking about something else, or of his having given up on the conversation. In these instances, the spouse's silence is hardly a matter of self-restraint. Silence counts as self-restraint only when we would like to say something but refrain from interrupting because refraining is what we think is best for the situation at the time. In other words, we are acting virtuously only when we are doing so intentionally, and for a worthy purpose.

Contrary to what we are often taught, cultivating virtue is not a matter of forcing ourselves to do things that we would rather not do. Developing virtue means becoming the kind of person who *wants* to act virtuously—someone who has a natural disposition to do what is best. That is why virtues are also called "character strengths." Virtues become part of our character, and the virtuous person naturally wants to do what is best. As we make virtue a part of us, our virtuous actions become spontaneous or second nature. The key to acquiring the disposition to act virtuously is to learn to love what is good; the desire to become a better person will follow naturally.

The kind of learning with which Aristotle is concerned is not just the mastery of information. It means gaining a real appreciation for the good and making what is good a part of us. Learning to skate is a good analogy. You can learn *information* about skating by talking with skaters, reading, or watching skaters, but if you want to skate, you must learn to do so by skating. What is more, you can learn to enjoy skating as an activity only by practicing and gaining skill. The better you become at skating, the more naturally you skate, and the more you enjoy it. You *become a skater* only by devoting yourself to skating. It is similar with virtue. We learn by practicing, we gain greater appreciation for virtue by enacting virtue, and we become virtuous by making virtue a part of us.

Aristotle believes that we can realize our essential human nature only to the extent that we cultivate good character. This view of humanity differs dramatically from the feel-good philosophies of self-development that are prevalent today. Contemporary views of self-development tend to focus on following our untutored emotions and impulses, as if doing what comes "naturally" were somehow magically right. Aristotle reminds us that pursuing worthy aims through virtuous action is more fully human than slavishly following our desires and impulses. According to Aristotle, we can truly flourish only by developing the moral excellence that is uniquely human. This means that we fulfill our nature by learning to follow our nobler feelings and inclinations instead of those that are base, by learning to practice decency rather than succumbing to the seductions of the dishonorable.

I am not suggesting that developing character will make us perfect. All of us make mistakes, have lapses in judgment, or occasionally just have a bad day. Attaining a virtuous disposition means only that we will be less likely to act basely and that we will recognize and more quickly correct the errors we do make. Cultivating virtue is about becoming a better person, not a perfect person.

Judgment

> *Anyone can get angry—that is easy . . . but to do*
> *this to the right person, to the right extent, at the right*
> *time, for the right reason, and in the right way is no*
> *longer something easy.*
>
> Aristotle[6]

Judgment, or practical wisdom, is a key to virtue, according to Aristotle, because we must continually make choices about how best to achieve what is good, and these choices are not always simple or straightforward. Exercising virtue requires the capacity to understand what is at stake in the endlessly varied situations we encounter, and to know how to foster the good in each circumstance. By *judgment*, I mean a reasoned or rational choice of the best option, considering the alternatives available in a situation.

For example, if you are having a disagreement with your partner, just how much self-restraint should you exercise? The appropriate degree of self-restraint will vary according to what is at issue between you (something important or something minor), the setting (private or public), your and your spouse's state of mind, and any number of other factors. You must make a judgment about how much to restrain the expression of your feelings and about how and when to share them.

Aristotle tells us that these kinds of judgments cannot be determined in advance and made into rules or routines spelling out when and how to exercise virtue. The noted philosopher Alasdair MacIntyre remarks that the absence of specific rules in Aristotle's *Nicomachean Ethics* is astonishing to modern readers, for we often think that ethical or moral action is based on rules that must be followed.[7] But Aristotle steadfastly holds that judgment must be exercised in each situation, and that rules can never be delineated in advance for all circumstances. Any moral rule or principle that we could devise would inevitably entail so many exceptions and qualifications that it would lose its force. Each exception would require its own rules, and these would also entail exceptions, which in turn would lead to an infinite proliferation of rules.

Aristotle offers us some guidance by defining virtues in terms of the golden mean. For each virtue, there are two attendant vices: the vice of excess, and the vice of deficiency. In a given situation, in other words, we can overdo any virtue, or we can exercise too little of it. For example, courage lies between rashness (excess) and timidity (deficiency); generosity is found between reckless giving and stinginess. Moreover, the appropriate exercise of a virtue will always vary according to the circumstances because the degree of self-restraint appropriate to one situation may be woefully inadequate to another and excessive in a third. This is why judgment is indispensable to virtue and shows us how courageous or restrained to be, given the circumstances.

What helps us know the best course of action in a given situation? One factor that aids judgment is a sense of what is at stake, or of what is crucial in the circumstances. Among the nearly infinite features of any situation, we have to be able to recognize what is important. The more clearly we see what the good is, the more clearly we can recognize what is at stake. For example, when an argument comes up in a marriage devoted to the ideal of partnership, the most important consideration is the maintenance of the partnership. It is important to resolve the problem, of course, and the spouses' expressions of their feelings do matter, but the prime consideration is for the spouses to find a way of working on the disagreement together, as partners.

A second factor that aids judgment is knowing which course of action is best, once you have recognized what is at stake in a particular situation. For example, your spouse may be very emotional about an issue and may not be in a position to think clearly with you. This situation may call for self-restraint and patience until your partner calms down. At another time, however, a misunderstanding may occur that can be resolved only if you let your partner know how something has hurt you. This kind of self-disclosure requires courage and honesty. In this way, recognizing what is important in a situation informs us about what we should do and guides us in knowing which virtues to emphasize.

It is not easy to determine what is best to do in the many morally complex situations we encounter. Aristotle gives us one ultimate guideline: to try to act as a wise person would, given the facts. When we think of what a wise person would do, we often think of exemplary people we know and take our cues from them. Fortunately for us, there are many wise people on whom we can model our actions. Because we are not born virtuous, and because there are no definitive rules for acting correctly, we all need heroes and guides who can offer us examples of how best to live. We can never fully master virtue and must be open to guidance and learning throughout our lives.

All of this may sound dauntingly complex and difficult, and you may wonder if it is even possible. Human life and relationships are indeed complex, and deciding what is best is frequently difficult. Moreover, we seldom have much certainty about whether we have made the best choices. One of the truly remarkable things about humans is that we do even as well as we do, given all this complexity and uncertainty. In any case, we have little choice except to try to do our best, and to learn from our inevitable mistakes. The truth is that you are continually making exactly the kinds of judgments we have been exploring here, and I am willing to bet that you make wise choices very frequently.

Discomfort with the Idea of Virtue

When it first occurred to me that the development and use of communication skills had to rely on a set of virtues, the insight seemed so obvious that I could not believe it wasn't common knowledge. But it took only a moment's thought for me to realize why the connection between communication skills and virtue has been neglected (and why it took me ten years to figure it out): many of us get nervous about discussing moral matters, such as virtue. We worry, for example, that we may be letting ourselves in for coercion by people with an authoritarian bent, who are all too eager to tell us what is right and good. We are much more comfortable with the idea that we can rely on dispassionate experts who use objective knowledge to help us reach our own freely chosen goals.

Our intellectual tradition encourages us, when we are dealing with moral matters, to cope with our anxiety about morality and authority by dividing the world into facts and values, into an objective and a subjective domain. The realm of objective facts is generally left to science, and to the experts who can apply it (therapists included). We have made questions of morality and value a matter of personal choice, in order to preserve our highly valued individual freedom.

The professional attempt to remain neutral on questions of value has failed because it is clear that there is simply no such thing as an objective expert when it comes to marriage. I have shown that social scientists and therapists are just as captivated as the rest of us are by the moral ideals of individualism and the myth of marital happiness. In other words, professionals are committed to the same contemporary cultural values as the general public rather than being detached in a way that reveals some sort of objective truth.

Moreover, the separation of facts from values, in spite of its usefulness, has created tremendous problems for us as we try to develop a workable understanding of morality. If we treat morality only as a matter of personal choice, then we undermine its ability to command our allegiance. If moral action really boils down to our individual choices, then why should we be bound by any code of conduct or vision of what is good? Why shouldn't we change our minds about what is right and good with every change in circumstances, or with every shift in our moods or whims?

But claiming possession of an objective truth about moral considerations smacks of arbitrariness and dogmatism. It is extremely difficult in our pluralistic, skeptical society to believe that we can attain any final truth about what is right or good. It does not help us to believe that morality is simply the product of social customs or norms, either. We are again faced with the same dilemma: any given moral claim appears to be either an offensive societal imposition or a mere habit subject to rejection or revision when it no longer serves our immediate individual desires.

It is important to respect the legitimate concerns that we have about discussions of shared morality. There is no shortage of people who want to tell us exactly what to believe and value. Defending ourselves from this kind of naked authoritarianism is one of the primary reasons we believe we must leave moral matters in the hands of individuals. But I think there is a third alternative beyond dogmatically imposed values and entirely subjective morality. I will discuss this alternative in the chapters that follow; for now, I will just say that we can have good reasons for committing ourselves to a shared morality even if we do not believe that we have the final truth.

I am convinced that there is no finality or certainty in matters of the human good. I certainly do not claim to have the last word. Even if we lack *ultimate* answers to questions about what is good in marriage, we can still find *good* answers. But, regardless of whether we feel that we have the final truth about marriage, we are always committed to some understanding of how to have a good marriage. Our commitment is evident in how we live our marriages. We may need to content ourselves with maintaining our allegiance to the best understanding of marriage that we can attain, without being able to lay claim to any ultimate truth.

6

The Virtue of Friendship

Building a Partnership Marriage

*No one would choose to live without friends, even if
he had all other goods.*

Aristotle[1]

As I have explored how virtue fits into marriage, I have been
guided by Aristotle's idea that virtues are the personal characteristics that make it possible for us to live the best kind of life.
That brings up one of the most important questions in all our lives:
What is the best kind of life? Of course, there is no ultimate answer
to that question that will fit for everyone, and our ideas about how
best to live may change over time. Nevertheless, all of us have some
concept of the kind of life we want to live and of how our marriages
fit into that picture. We may not always be able to put our visions
of the good life into words, but our ideals show up in what we see
as important and in what we try to accomplish.

We saw in Chapter Two that having a happy marriage is virtually necessary to feeling good about our lives in contemporary
America. One of the most widely held beliefs in our society is that
being happily married to someone we consider a friend is a crucial
part of the good life. Let's look into how friendship can be an important aspect of marriage.

What Is Friendship in Marriage?

Exploring Aristotle's thoughts about friendship has helped me clarify my understanding of how to foster enduring, vibrant marriages. In its most important aspects, his understanding of friendship is as relevant and enlivening today as it was in his own time, even though it differs from contemporary ideas about friendship. For Aristotle, friendship is central to all social arrangements, from households to cities, but he thinks that family relationships are the original and, in many ways, central instances of friendship.

Virtually everyone believes that spouses should be friends, and a guiding ideal for many partners is to be each other's best friend. The word *friend* has many connotations: fondness, caring, intimacy, allegiance, support, helpfulness, companionship, and trust, to name a few. As we have seen, many people believe that being good friends means that they listen to and understand each other. Oftentimes we think of friendship in terms of having fun together and enjoying one another's company. In other words, we think of friendship primarily in emotional terms, as a matter of mutual attachment and liking, support, and sympathy.

The idea that friendship is primarily an emotional bond that is based on sharing good feelings is very attractive, isn't it? Being friends with your spouse can broaden and deepen your relationship in important ways. Many people believe that being friends with their spouses makes their marriages stronger. There is certainly some truth to this idea, but there is an important problem with building our marriages around the ordinary concept of friendship. The difficulty is that friendships that are based solely on mutual emotional enjoyment are only as durable as the emotional benefits they provide. Because our feelings are so changeable, an attachment based only on our feelings for someone can be quite fragile.

If a relationship is no more than an emotional attachment between two people, whether that attachment is based on romantic love or on being friends, the relationship can last only as long as the good feelings do. In that case, being friends, even the best of friends, with our spouses does not change the prevailing formula that dictates that a good marriage is one in which the spouses have good feelings toward each other. Modern marriages are fragile largely because we expect so much from them emotionally, and because our commitment to our marriages is so dependent on whether they make us feel good. If the only basis for our friendships with our spouses is our feelings, then these friendships can sour, just as romantic love can. Our friendships with our spouses are vulnerable to the shifting sands of our emotions, just as our feelings of happiness in romance-based marriages are. For this reason, we need to identify an alternative to emotionally focused friendship in marriage.

Aristotle's Three Forms of Friendship

Aristotle clarifies our understanding of friendship by distinguishing three types of friendships. He describes *advantage friendships* (those characterized by mutual benefit) and *pleasure friendships* (those involving mutual pleasure) as the two most common kinds of relationships. He calls the third (and best) kind of friendship a *character* or virtue friendship because it is based on the friends' recognition of each other's good character and on the shared pursuit of worthy goals. Friends of all three types share some goals, and all three types of friends are interested in helping each other. All friendships involve wanting the best for your friend and doing what you can to bring that about. Naturally, a friend would reciprocate this interest. The differences among the three types of friendship come in what leads the friends to like each other and in the nature of the commitment that the friends have to each other.

Advantage and Pleasure Friendships

Advantage friendships are based on the mutual benefits the friends provide for each other. The best examples of this kind of friendship can be found in business or political circles. People in business frequently cultivate and maintain friendships that are based on helping one another further their business interests. This is usually mutually understood and does not necessarily involve manipulation or just "using" one another. These friendships often involve genuine positive feelings, which are enhanced by the friends' helping each other in business. Marriages that are based primarily on economic or social benefits are a kind of advantage friendship.

Pleasure friendships have a similar basis, but the friends offer one another enjoyment rather than advantage (although the two types of friendships are not mutually exclusive). The gratifications found in pleasure friendships can vary widely, including such experiences as simple enjoyment of each other's company, mutual involvement in a hobby, a shared appreciation for art, sexual pleasure, and so on. Many of our friendships take this form; we are friends simply because we like each other, and it is pleasant to be together.

It is good to have advantage and pleasure friendships, but these kinds of relationships have serious limitations that are particularly relevant to marriage. One important drawback is that advantage and pleasure friendships tend to be primarily self-serving in their emphasis on receiving enjoyment or benefits. There is no necessary connection between what is advantageous or pleasurable to someone and any larger benefits or purposes. Advantage and pleasure friendships could have wider benefits, but that would be more by happenstance than by design. Another difficulty is that these two types of friendship last only as long as the mutual advantage or pleasure endures. For example, if a business associate ceases to be useful, and if the friendship hasn't taken on a significant alternative basis, such as the friends' coming to really enjoy each other's company, then it is very likely that the friendship will fade.

The brittle character of modern marriage is entirely consistent with Aristotle's recognition that relationships based on advantage or pleasure endure only as long as they remain beneficial to the participants. In fact, while I was writing this chapter, I heard about several marriages that ended because one of the partners simply ceased to find sufficient advantage or pleasure in the relationship and wanted out.

One soon-to-be ex-wife, Lisa, decided unilaterally to divorce her husband, John, because she felt that she needed more excitement and passion in her life. She announced her decision to him one day as a fait accompli. John, naturally enough, was shocked and hurt, but he could not persuade Lisa to reconsider. She is now pursuing a divorce.

There was universal shock and surprise in Lisa's social circle because she is a well-educated, hardworking dance instructor and the loving mother of three children. She is not a frivolous, devil-may-care person; she is someone who in many ways has shown the capacity for commitment and caring. How is it that she could just walk out of a ten-year marriage in this way? Her leaving her husband follows logically from the contemporary belief that the central aim of marriage is the provision of pleasure, enjoyment, and satisfaction. Many people may criticize Lisa for her decision, but it is rather unreasonable to fault someone for following a prevalent cultural script.

Unfortunately, Lisa and John's experience is not terribly unusual. Our popular and professional understanding of marriage takes it for granted that a good marriage is based on some combination of mutual pleasure and benefit. Seeing marriage primarily in terms of its benefits to the individual spouses is the core of the myth of marital happiness. The high frequency of divorce is a natural consequence of this widely shared understanding. Aristotle's notion of character friendship is one well worth exploring because it offers a clear alternative to the instability inherent in advantage- and pleasure-based marriages.

Character Friendships

There are three qualities of character friendships that distinguish them from pleasure and advantage friendships. First, character friends share an understanding of what is good or worthy and a mutual commitment to seeking it. Second, they are brought together because they recognize each other's good qualities—the character strengths that make it possible for them to seek the good together. Third, character friends work together as a team or a partnership to achieve their shared goals.

Character friendship is also pleasurable and beneficial, but it transcends these considerations. In other words, the nature of the friendship goes beyond the individual interests or enjoyment of the friends and aims at larger goals. In a character friendship, mutual happiness is a by-product of shared commitment and teamwork rather than the primary goal. There is no one right kind of marriage, because there are so many different aims or projects that couples may find worthy, but the common theme is the spouses' working together to build a shared life. These projects or goals could include cultivating the kind of family life that encourages children to become responsible, flourishing adults, or advancing some area of human excellence such as literature or athletics, or enriching the social and political life of the community, or many other worthy pursuits.

But let me sharpen the contrast between advantage and pleasure friendships and character friendships in marriage. Benefit-based relationships do involve cooperation, and the spouses in a character marriage do enjoy positive feelings about the relationship. The difference is in where we place the most emphasis or in how we define the core of the relationship. Whereas relationships based on benefit are sustained primarily by the material goods or pleasurable emotions that the partners experience with each other, character marriages are based more on shared goals and on cooperative efforts to reach them. The shared goals that make a character marriage a partnership represent a mutual endeavor, beyond the couple's relationship, that can help sustain the marriage.

Affection is important in friendship and marriage, of course, but Aristotle reminds us that it is a by-product of a more important bond, which is forged through the development of shared goals.

Marital teamwork is directed toward goals or ideals that go beyond the feelings the partners have for each other, but the couple's aims still include and enrich their feelings for each other. When spouses work cooperatively toward some end, or to fulfill some purpose, their cooperation draws them together and enhances their emotional experience. At the same time, their shared goals give their relationship a direction and a significance that transcends their emotional experience.

Remember Wendy and Al, the couple we met in Chapter Two, who decided to start a business marketing Native American art? They created a business because they shared a deep interest, and they wanted to make Native American art available to others. Their business is the embodiment of a set of shared goals that have given their marriage a new dimension. Working together to choose and market art deepens their emotional attachment, but this project is larger than their feelings for each other, and it ties them to the community of people who create and patronize Native American art. This shared project has helped them prosper in their marriage.

Character Friendship and Marriage

The best friendships are those characterized by shared goals, the partners' recognition of each other's good qualities, and teamwork. These three features of a character friendship capture some of the most important aspects of a strong marriage. Exploring these aspects of character friendship can help you recognize and appreciate aspects of your marriage that are neglected by the vast majority of books and articles on marriage. In addition, understanding character friendship in marriage can help you cultivate these sources of strength and vibrancy for your marriage.

Shared Goals

The first aspect of a character friendship is shared goals. Character friends are brought together largely by their shared view of what is good in life. The most common way that couples express this is in saying that they have the same goals or that they want the same things out of life. A strong marriage is built on shared aims that provide a kind of blueprint for the marriage. Of course, that does not mean that all couples can spell out their goals explicitly. Many couples do not articulate what they find important in life, but their shared aims are apparent in their perspectives on life and in the activities they pursue. Spouses may or may not be able to tell you what their goals are, but if you are observant, you can recognize what is important to them by how they act. Let's look into some examples of the various goals that help define different couples' marriages.

Amy and Martin both come from families in which music is very important. They both love music very much. They recognized musical inclination and talent in their children from an early age and started them in musical training. Amy and the children get up early to practice their music every day before school. The children do not need to be pushed into practicing and performing because they love music, too. They teach themselves to play new instruments, and they form their own bands with friends. Martin is also actively involved, taking the children to music lessons and encouraging their excellence. A considerable proportion of the family's income is devoted to musical training and instruments. Music is a constant presence in the house, and it feels almost magical to the family.

Amy and Martin have always wanted their home to be a musical one, and they have made it so by playing instruments themselves and teaching their children to be musical. Even though it was not always a consciously held goal, they believe that cultivating their children's talent is a very worthy pursuit, and they have arranged their schedules and finances to facilitate this endeavor. Their efforts were rewarded recently, when their eldest daughter was selected as the best cellist in the state for her age group. Devoting themselves to their children's talent has enriched their relationship by providing a shared goal and by making their home ring with the music they love. Amy and Martin show how shared goals enhance a relationship. They share great pride and joy in their children's developing talent, but their efforts with their children do not crowd out or replace their mutual affection. They also enjoy each other's company in weekly dates and in time spent together at home.

I have been most impressed with the work of former President Jimmy Carter and former First Lady Rosalynn Carter. As I have learned more about their activities, I have been just as fascinated by the partnership that they have built in their marriage of over fifty years. Their partnership began inauspiciously in Plains, Georgia, where they both grew up. They knew each other, as everyone knows everyone else in a small town. Rosalynn was a friend of Jimmy's sister Ruth, and in their teenage years the two girls schemed to get Rosalynn together with Jimmy. Nothing came of these plans for a long time, but one day Jimmy decided to ask Rosalynn to see a movie with him. They had a very nice time, and even though nothing extraordinary had happened, Jimmy told his mother that someday he would marry Rosalynn.

When Jimmy went off to the U.S. Naval Academy, he and Rosalynn corresponded. When he came back home for Christmas, he proposed, and she turned him down because she had promised her father she would get a college education. He persevered, and she accepted his second proposal. They had a small wedding and went off to live as a navy couple.

In the early years of their marriage, Jimmy was very much in charge. He tended to keep his thoughts and feelings to himself, and when he was troubled by something, Rosalynn feared he was angry with her. Her distress only upset him more, and it was difficult for them to communicate in those years. When his father was dying, Jimmy decided on his own to return to Plains to take over the family business. Rosalynn was furious because she was very happy with their life as it was. She did not want to return to the small town where her newfound independence might be undermined by their mothers and by the pressures of small-town life. They fought loudly about it: Rosalynn insisted that they stay with the navy, but Jimmy was adamant about returning to Plains. Jimmy resigned his commission, and they had a silent drive from New York to Georgia.

As they worked to build the family business, Jimmy came to rely on Rosalynn more. Her independence and talents began to show through. As Jimmy began his political career, her advice and participation became increasingly important. He said, "When we decided to enter politics, Rosalynn helped me from every standpoint. We have been full partners in every major decision."[2] This partnership was a full-blown one during Jimmy Carter's presidency, and the president's advisers were well aware of the influence Rosalynn had on him, and of the importance of her support and guidance. She was not simply a passive companion; she worked with her husband as his eyes and ears and as his most trusted counselor.[3]

The period following Jimmy Carter's reelection defeat was naturally very difficult for them both. The voters' apparent repudiation of the agenda for peace and human rights that they had so ardently pursued was particularly painful. He also discovered at this time that the family business, which he had placed in a blind trust during his presidency, was virtually bankrupt. This difficult period, as the Carters struggled through it, actually helped bring them closer as a couple.

They began to write a book together that was eventually called *Everything to Gain*. Their collaboration on this book severely strained their relationship because they had very different writing styles and could not agree on some of the points they were making. Rosalynn writes very carefully and wants things to be just right, whereas Jimmy writes more quickly and casually. Their disputes became very heated at times. Finally, their publisher divided up paragraphs of the book, and they wrote them independently, identifying them with a J or an R. Jimmy says they could not agree on anything at that time; they would fight about the bedroom temperature, with Rosalynn feeling cold while he felt hot. He went on a trip, worried that his marriage might be destroyed. When he returned, Rosalynn greeted him with a smile and said she had the solution to their problem. He was not sure what to expect, but she told him that they had had their electric blanket hooked up backwards, so that when she tried to raise the temperature, she cooked him, and when he tried to lower it, he froze her. This simple resolution helped pave the way for a broader reconciliation.

At the Carter Center, Jimmy and Rosalynn work very closely together on some projects, but they have independent projects as well. Whether they are deeply involved with each other's work or only serving as each other's occasional adviser, they see themselves as partners in the most complete sense of the term. Jimmy has said that the Carter Center is the realization of their shared dream to promote human rights and wage peace. Rosalynn is a conspicuous and active participant in the peace negotiations that have relieved so much misery and saved so many lives, as well as in the election monitoring that has helped make democracy a reality in many places. Jimmy assists her efforts with caregivers of the elderly and her promotion of mental health services. Their joint participation as volunteers with Habitat for Humanity has brought that worthy organization much-needed and well-deserved attention and contributions.

The Carters' fifty-plus years of partnership and accomplishment are very inspiring. They have worked together to bring about their dreams, both in public and in private life. Their lives have not been easy, and their marriage has not been free of conflict. At times they have had epic battles that lasted for weeks, but their commitment to each other, to their faith, and to their shared projects has carried them through these difficult times. Their lives have been devoted to a shared vision of the good that they have actively promoted for themselves, their descendants, and humanity.

The Carters' is an inspiring but unusual way of life; other couples become involved in community life in less demanding but no less important ways. An older couple I know provides a good example. Allison and Max are both retired and have developed what I think is an admirable character friendship. They have been married for twelve years, and both have grown children from previous marriages. They both have a keen interest in the cultural and community life of their city. This interest is expressed through their memberships in local museums and their subscriptions to the symphony and the opera company.

Allison and Max go beyond simply enjoying these activities, however. Both of them are actively involved in promoting cultural and civic events through volunteer work. They enjoy their participation in these events, and doing this work together increases their pleasure in it. More important, however, they know that without volunteers like them, the cultural life of their city would be severely impoverished. Their shared commitment to their community not only has enriched their marriage but is also a contribution to a vibrant community life.

The most important feature of the character friendships exemplified by these three couples is the partners' joint commitment to goals that go beyond their relationship as a couple. Having a personal commitment to your spouse and to the enjoyment of your marriage is a very good thing, but it can be unstable. When a couple is devoted to life projects that transcend their relationship, they incorporate a much stronger and more stable form of commitment than what is available only through emotional involvement. This kind of commitment is more stable because the kinds of goals that guide us throughout our lives are themselves stable, and they give our individual and married lives a deep sense of meaning.

Because a shared sense of what is worthwhile is important, it is clear that one of the most important issues in the decision to marry has to be the prospective spouses' genuine compatibility in life goals. Many partners assume that their aims in life will be naturally compatible simply because they love each other. In some cases it works out this way, but more than a decade of research and clinical observations with engaged and married couples has led me to the conclusion that an initial incompatibility is much more likely to result in serious, unresolved conflict and divorce than in a magical unification through mutual attraction. The fantasy that love conquers all is an important part of the myth of marital happiness, and it is pervasive among many of the engaged couples I have interviewed. Even when they tell me in unmistakable ways that their relationship is troubled, they have an almost unshakable belief that once they are married, all their troubles will melt away. This fantasy is encouraged by our romantic faith in the power of love.

The Mutual Recognition of Good Qualities

The second aspect of a character friendship is that the partners recognize in each other the character strengths that are necessary to bring about the goals they share. In other words, they love each other partly because they share an understanding of what is good and partly because they recognize the personal strengths in each other that are necessary to bring their aims to life. This kind of friendship develops when two people spend enough time together that each comes to know the other's character and comes to love the other because of his or her good qualities. We see that our friend is someone with whom we can pursue important goals. Character friends love each other for those essential good characteristics, not simply because the friend incidentally offers pleasurable company or some kind of advantage.

This is the basis of the proverb that we are known by the company we keep. Our character is revealed by whom we choose as friends and spouses, partly because the nature of these friendships shows what is important to us. For example, if we are interested in social status, we will likely choose friends who have the personal characteristics that lend themselves to gaining and holding social position. These friendship choices say a lot about how much we value social status.

The strongest marriages I have seen are based on character friendships in which the partners clearly recognize each other's strengths. In these marriages, the couple's identity is strongly imbued with the idea that the spouses are in a partnership that may involve some sacrifice but that helps give their marriage greater meaning and strength.

For example, Kim and Paul have been married for seven years. When they decided to have a third baby, Kim developed some unexpected complications with her pregnancy. She felt particularly worn out and unable to keep up with her work schedule and the household chores. If she tried to follow anything like her ordinary routine, she began to experience serious contractions and spotting.

Paul was willing to take on the chores that Kim could not manage around the house, and he increased his time with their son and their daughter. This meant that Paul had to cut back on his time with his friends and on his beloved scuba diving. I asked him how he felt about these sacrifices, and he told me that he wished Kim were not having trouble with the pregnancy, but that they had decided together to have another baby. He could not help her carry the baby to term, but he could make that a little easier for her by doing more at home.

Paul said he did not mind the small sacrifices he was making, because this pregnancy was important to both of them, and it was something they were doing together. In other words, having another baby was a shared goal that was just one aspect of their partnership. We would hope that all fathers-to-be would do what Paul did, but Kim believes that Paul's character really shows in that he *gladly* did more than usual for the sake of their mutual goal. To do extra work grudgingly suggests a lack of choice, whereas cheerfully doing what is necessary demonstrates willing participation in something worthwhile.

Teamwork

The third aspect of a character friendship is that the friends develop mutual understanding of their roles in bringing about their aims. Spouses who have character friendships cooperate in the mundane tasks of everyday life as well as in their larger goals. There is an infinite variety of possible arrangements, from the traditional homemaker-breadwinner division of labor to a more egalitarian, flexible partnership in which decisions and tasks are accomplished by one or both partners in whatever way is most advantageous. The particular arrangement of who does what is often less important than the shared understanding of what needs to be done and of how each person can contribute.

Because teamwork in accomplishing shared goals is such an important part of a character friendships, I will refer from now on to marriages based on character friendships as *partnerships* or *partnership marriages*. I also like to think of spouses as partners, in the full sense of the term: as people committed to joint projects and purposes.

Let me illustrate this aspect of a partnership marriage with a couple, Sheri and Bob, who have focused their energies on the important aim of raising their children well. From the beginning of their marriage, Sheri and Bob have agreed that their central goal is to cultivate a family life in which their children can feel secure and receive proper guidance. The larger good for them is to raise their children to become flourishing, contributing adults who carry on the civic and religious traditions of their family. Accordingly, they have made career and financial decisions that have allowed them to create the family life they seek.

Bob is a professor with a flexible schedule, and Sheri is a physical therapist. She works in the mornings, and some evenings, so that she can be with the children in the afternoons. In this way, at least one of them is with the children after school, at dinner, and at bedtime, even though both of them must work some evenings. They share household tasks in a similar way, from the morning routine (Bob makes breakfast, Sheri makes lunch) to taking care of finances (he does monthly finances, she does the taxes). Each has gravitated toward the tasks for which he or she is best suited, and, as necessary, they switch tasks or work together on chores. They both recognize what needs to be done, and they each pitch in to take care of the children and the chores or to arrange dates for the two of them, without paying attention to whose turn it is to do this or that. Their commitment to their shared goals, in addition to their faith in each other's willingness to contribute, allows them to participate fully in building and maintaining their chosen life.

This arrangement does have some drawbacks, of course. Sheri and Bob explain that restrictions in Sheri's working hours, along with Bob's decision to forgo consulting income, mean that they live in a modest home and do not take lavish vacations. Their schedules are often rather hectic, and they have to coordinate them from week to week. They find great comfort, however, in the feeling that they are working together to accomplish a worthy goal. When I asked them whether they are ever unhappy about the career and financial sacrifices they are making, they said that from time to time they do bemoan these sacrifices. At these times, they recall together the reasons why they made their choices, and doing this reminds them of the worthiness of their goals, relieves their temporary discontent, and reaffirms their efforts.

Sheri and Bob exemplify one way to have a partnership marriage, one that is guided by a particular set of goals and ideals. As we have seen, however, there are many ways to have a good marriage. The unifying theme among the many different goals that the partners may have is the idea that marriage is ultimately about building a shared life. One reason why marriage works for Sheri and Bob is that they agree on which goals and purposes to pursue together. Their success is also dependent on each spouse doing his or her part. Becoming partners in any real sense means that the spouses agree about what is most important to them in their lives and then work together to bring those values to life. It sounds simple enough, but it is not necessarily easy to reach agreement about the best way to live together, nor can we take it for granted that we will be able to pursue our shared values smoothly once we have reached consensus about what our values should be. Agreement with your partner on the kind of life you want together cannot be taken for granted. It may take some sustained work, but the added depth and durability of a partnership marriage is well worth the effort.

Finding Common Ground

The partnership approach to marriage became crystal clear to me in doing therapy with couples. One of the most common aspects of distressed couples is that the partners cannot find common ground or cooperate, even in small ways. Some couples have, at best, the maturity to cooperate in managing the basic necessities of life, even though they are otherwise unhappy with one another, but their partnership usually extends no farther. This led me to focus on helping couples to think of themselves as a partnership or team. In my experience, the search for common ground and the development of teamwork are a very large and beneficial part of marital therapy.

I learned an important lesson about teamwork very early in my marriage. My wife and I were having one of those inevitable disagreements about something. (Who can ever remember what those things were about?) We were both busily arguing our separate points of view, but then Susan became quiet for a moment. When my curiosity finally slowed me down, Susan asked, "Can we be on the same side here?" How could I say no? Her question stopped me in my tracks and transformed that argument into a discussion of how *we* were going to solve a problem that *we shared*. We became partners in working something out rather than fighting with each other over it because we both wanted to be on the same side more than we wanted to win the argument. Our shared understanding that we are working together to solve any difficulties we face has helped us immensely, even when the problem is that we disagree with each other. The idea of our being on the same side reminds us that our marriage is more important than almost any disagreements we might have.

Susan and I are not in agreement about everything, of course, and sometimes we come together simply by agreeing to disagree. We are willing to tolerate differences between us because we recognize that we are individuals with different histories and perspectives, and agreeing to disagree is another way that we commit ourselves to our partnership. In other words, we do not necessarily insist that we agree on everything, because some differences cannot be resolved, and pursuing agreement may be destructive to the partnership. Complete consensus is not necessary to a good marriage.

Many marital educators and therapists are fond of teaching conflict-resolution skills or problem-solving steps for dealing with disagreements. There is no doubt that identifying the problem, brainstorming, and using the other problem-solving steps can sometimes be useful. But conflict-resolution procedures are effective only if the spouses are willing to work together; otherwise, the procedures just provide something else to argue about. If you and your partner are able to work together on the problem, then the problem-solving steps may be helpful, but you also may not need them. If you can't work together, then the steps alone certainly won't help. I think the primary benefit of problem-solving techniques is that they show couples one way for them to be on the same side—but why not focus in the first place on teamwork, which is the most crucial aspect of conflict resolution?

The Virtue of Friendship in Marriage

Fully embracing the ideal of a partnership marriage means that you *want* to have shared goals, and that you *want* to work with your spouse to bring your goals about. When you come to love an ideal, such as partnership, you do not have to force yourself to be a partner against your inclinations. Because cultivating virtue means developing a disposition to act virtuously, you freely and ungrudgingly do what is best. Of course, you may not want to act as a partner occasionally, and you may even question the value of your partnership at times. It is only human to be conflicted from time to time about doing what we believe to be best, and to struggle with ourselves. But if you fully embrace the ideal of partnership, you will, in the main, find yourself exercising the virtue of friendship naturally and willingly because you want to have the partnership more than you want to prevail in an argument or get the better of your spouse. Occasionally you may need to rise above a base inclination to hurt or take advantage of your partner; on reflection, however, you will gladly make the nobler choice. To someone committed to a partnership, the satisfaction of winning or of being in a one-up position seems hollow and unworthy most of the time. In other words, the things that get in the way of the partnership simply cease to be desirable.

Even if both partners are committed to a partnership marriage, they will still experience disagreements. Differences will always arise and should be worked out. When you are committed to a partnership, however, the point of the argument is not getting your way or hurting one another; it is looking for a way to work together in solving the problem. This involves finding common ground—finding a way to be on the same side, to see a problem as something that you share rather than as something that divides you as a couple. In a partnership marriage, the marriage is more important than almost any problem. Practicing the virtue of friendship illustrates how learning to love the good can change our desires so that what we want becomes consistent with what is good. That is why having character means that you do not have to force yourself to act virtuously.

The ideal of a marriage based on a character friendship is certainly not a magic bullet. The ideal of a partnership marriage will not eliminate marital discord or even divorce. Some couples may find it almost impossible to develop a character friendship—their goals in life are too different, the spouses do not admire each other's personal qualities, or the spouses cannot find a way to work as a team. Some of these couples may be able to maintain their marriages as pleasure or advantage friendships. But there are other couples in whose marriages common ground is almost entirely lacking, as is any ability for them to be civil with each other, much less work as a team. Unfortunately, for any or all of these reasons, some marriages are not sustainable.

The best approach to such problems is to avoid this predicament in the first place by choosing your mate wisely. The importance of character friendship suggests that it is wise to choose a mate with whom we share some key life goals. It is also easy to see the importance of marrying someone who is capable of pursuing those aims with us and who demonstrates a commitment to them. Another way to prevent the deterioration of a marriage is to remember that disaffection and estrangement seldom appear suddenly. It is far more common for us to let the repetition of small disagreements and differences gradually drive a wedge between us, or for us to hold on to grudges and disappointments that undermine our willingness to work together as a team. In this way, marriages that begin very well deteriorate until they are no longer tolerable to the spouses.

It is essential that we understand the centrality of partnership in marriage, and that we work to maintain our ability to be on the same side as our spouses, even when we disagree. We have to protect our bonds with our partners, work together to resolve the inevitable conflicts that arise, and deal with the endless round of mundane activities in everyday life. Practicing self-restraint, exercising courage, being generous, and using good judgment in our interactions with our partners will help us foster character friendships and partnership marriages.

All of us would agree with Aristotle that friendship is indispensable to living well. We would even agree with him that marriage at its best is a relationship built on friendship. Expanding your understanding of friendship beyond mutual pleasure and mutual benefit can go a long way toward strengthening your marriage. By doing so, you can enhance your enjoyment of your marriage and expand the benefits that you receive from it. Pursuing shared aims enriches a relationship in many ways. It brings a deeper form of togetherness than can be provided by emotional intimacy through communication alone. Sharing activities with your spouse will help reinforce your mutual interests and contribute to your feeling that these activities are worthwhile. Sharing activities with your spouse also helps connect you as individuals with your broader community, whether through play groups, the PTA, religious organizations, civic groups, or political activity.

I chose friendship as the first virtue to discuss in depth because I think that virtue friendship provides a clear alternative to the individual gratification approach to marriage. By developing partnerships, we can enrich and strengthen our marriages. Cultivating the virtue of friendship may take some effort, but these exertions will be richly rewarded by having a better marriage and by becoming a better person.

Practicing the virtue of friendship (as well as practicing the other virtues I discuss in subsequent chapters) is not just about marriage. Because our character strengths go with us into all aspects of our lives, what is good for our marriages is also good for our other endeavors. Conversely, because there is no clear boundary between our lives as spouses and our lives as employees, citizens, or friends, one of the best ways to have good, strong marriages is for us to become better people in all aspects of our lives.

The virtues I am discussing in this book are oriented toward pursuing goods in life that are held in common with others, whether the virtues are practiced in marriages, other friendships, or in the community. Friendship obviously involves another person, but the shared nature of character friendship goes even farther because character friendship can only be developed if you and your friend have common goals and ideals. We will discuss loyalty, generosity, and justice in the coming chapters. These virtues are also practiced within relationships and oriented toward the attainment of shared goals. Indeed, partnership virtues become meaningless without a partner, friend, or fellow citizen toward whom we can practice them. This emphasis on being good with and toward your partner is a crucial way that partnership marriage differs from the predominant story of marriage as beneficial to individual spouses.

7

The Virtue of Loyalty

Creating a Lasting Marriage

Chains do not hold a marriage together. It is threads,
hundreds of tiny threads which sew people together
through the years. That is what makes a marriage
last—more than passion or even sex!

Simone Signoret[1]

In today's fast-paced, gratification-oriented consumer society, it can be more surprising when a marriage lasts a lifetime than when it ends in divorce. The pressures of having both partners working outside the home, the emotional needs of growing children, the carpooling required for children's activities, the lure of various entertainments, and involvements with friends and family pull spouses in many different directions and threaten marriages with fragmentation. What can hold marriages together in the face of so many pressures and demands?

The myth of marital happiness tells us that the emotional benefits of marriage, such as satisfaction, intimacy, or mutual gratification, form the primary glue that holds couples together. Our excessive focus on emotional fulfillment has made us more prone to disappointment with our marriages and more likely to divorce. But if happiness cannot create stronger marriages, what can?

In this chapter, I will highlight the powerful loyalty to our partners that grows naturally out of our living and working together. This loyalty is deeper and richer than our conscious decisions and more fundamental to us than our emotions. Loyalty grows organically as our lives are intertwined with others and as our identities are shaped by our relationships with them. It is one of the most profound sources of our ties to our partners.

Loyalty and Identity

In the way we draw the lines of our loyalties, we define ourselves as persons.

George Fletcher[2]

We are sometimes surprised by the powerful loyalties we feel toward our family members, the cultural groups to which we belong, and our nation. We are often profoundly moved by allegiances that may be difficult to explain fully to ourselves or to others. Children offer a profound degree of loyalty to their parents. This filial loyalty is most striking when it seems least justified, as in abusive families. We are all aware of the irony in the fact that siblings fight endlessly with each other but indignantly defend each other from assaults by anyone outside the family. Patriotism is another important example of a strong attachment that most of us absorb rather than choose explicitly. Loyalty is a very powerful bond that is a significant part of all of our lives. How do we acquire these powerful feelings, almost without realizing it?

We are loyal to the people and institutions that shape our individual identity. The bonds we feel toward our families, our country, and our cultures are based on the fact that participating in these entities makes us who we are. Let's explore how loyalty to others is related to attaining identity as an individual, in order to set the stage for understanding the place of loyalty in marriage.

The Origins of Loyalty

History does not belong to us; we belong to it.
                                        Hans Georg Gadamer[3]

The extreme form of individualism in our culture makes it difficult for us to recognize how deeply our individual lives and identities are shaped by our participation in our particular families, educational settings, occupations, cultural groups, religious groups, nations, and so forth. In our preoccupation with the separateness and independence of individuals, we seriously underestimate the degree to which we become who we are because we live in our particular communities and in our particular nation.

In his wonderful book, *Loyalty*, George Fletcher points out that we feel a deep attachment toward the people and groups with whom we share a significant history. He calls this experience *loyalty*.[4] We tend to be partial or biased toward those with whom we live and toward those with whom we have shared important experiences. Loyalty is not general or abstract. It arises only in the specific relationships we have with other individuals or with the groups to which we belong. We also develop feelings of loyalty to people with whom we associate as adults, and marriage is a particularly important arena where loyalty grows.

Our loyalties are always historical. We become committed to people, groups, and ideals gradually, by sharing a significant history during which our identity is shaped or reshaped. This reshaping of individual identity almost always occurs over time, through ongoing engagement with someone or something. Our loyalty to our families grows out of years of upbringing. Our loyalty to our country develops through decades of instruction, ritual, and pageantry. Our loyalty to our alma mater is due to our attendance during a crucial time of maturation and to our alma mater's rivalry with other schools. We are loyal to those with whom we have shared a significant past because our shared history helps make us who we are. *We are loyal to our families and our nation because they are part of us.*

The philosopher Martin Heidegger has some compelling insights into how our identities are formed by our social world.[5] When we are born, we enter a social world that was complete before we arrived. This world surrounds us from our birth and forms the background and basis of all of our thoughts, feelings, and actions. It is a world richly endowed with meanings and commitments, many of which we inherit by being born into it.

A large part of raising a child is teaching the child to operate in and through the customs, values, and expectations of the family and the cultural group. This learning begins almost from the moment of birth and is very advanced before any of us has a chance to choose what we will learn and whether we want to accept the social world that is shaping us. The understandings, customs, and practices of our cultural group are a kind of cultural atmosphere that we take in with every breath because it surrounds us continually. We feel at home in our social world because we are woven into it.

At birth, a person becomes, for example, a male Wilson who is an American Roman Catholic of English descent. All of these identifiers carry meanings and commitments that are rooted in generations of family, religion, and politics. We almost automatically absorb all these facts and their significance early in life. A significant part of our identities is conferred on us at birth. We like to think that we choose who we become, but being born in a particular family, culture, and time defines our lives in a very real and profound (but not complete) way.

The easiest way to see just how dependent each of us is on our social context is to think about all we have to learn in order to become functioning adults. Newborns are really marvelous beings, and we have learned that they influence their caretakers much more than we used to think: through maintaining or ending eye contact, through expressions of excitement, and through a surprising variety of cries. A normal newborn comes with all the potential for growing into a complete human being, given time, care, and guidance. Yet the sheer volume of information and skills that children must learn to actually become fully human is mind-boggling. Infants have the physiological equipment that prepares them to talk, but they must learn from their caretakers and peers how to use an actual language. They are primed for a social way of life, but they must learn how to manage the nearly infinite variety of social situations in a particular culture.

Contrary to the conventional wisdom that we become our "genuine" selves by resisting the influence of our social world, Heidegger tells us that our membership in a social group is not a limitation or a burden on our individuality. Instead, being a member of a social group actually enables us to become human in the first place. We can obtain a real sense of substantial, meaningful identity only through participation in a social group. If we lacked this cultural background, we would not be free spirits or more authentic people; we would be disoriented and impoverished, with no coherent direction for our lives.

We do not begin life as independent individuals who adopt a cultural way of life in the same way we put on clothing. It is really just the opposite. Our cultural surroundings give our identities and our lives their original shape and direction. We can modify the contours of our lives through our choices and actions, but we cannot remake our lives from scratch, entirely as we choose. Being an authentic person is not a matter of throwing off our cultural shells and freeing our inner nature. It is a matter of learning how to live out our cultural possibilities in a richer, more focused way.

As we mature and begin to reflect on our place in our social world, we recognize that it is possible to disagree with things that we usually take for granted. We do have some degree of freedom because the choices we make give our lives a particular shape. On the one hand, we inevitably draw these choices from the culturally given possibilities available to us, and so we are always tied to our cultural upbringing. On the other hand, we can reinterpret what we have inherited, to create new prospects for living. Our "nature" as humans is not something that we can entirely make through our own choices, nor is it something we simply find in our social world or our inner selves. Instead, in the words of my friend Charles Guignon, our lives become "what we make of what we find."

The Depth of Loyalty

We express our loyalties in every waking moment by the ways we think, feel, and act because our experiences and actions are always informed by our cultural background. When I think, feel, or act like an American, like a Fowers, or like a psychologist, I am expressing loyalty to the country, family, and profession that have helped make me the person I am. I don't usually do this consciously. It happens all by itself because those influences are aspects of my identity. Wearing a watch and being aware of the time is an act of loyalty to our time-conscious culture. Striving to succeed as an individual is an expression of loyalty to our achievement-oriented, individualistic culture. We generally act on and embody our loyalties without thinking about them, because doing so comes naturally. It simply makes sense to us to act in accordance with our social customs.

The loyalties we experience to our families, cultures, and nation are not merely psychological. We do experience loyalty psychologically, of course, but our loyalties run much, much deeper. Our attachments to our families, cultures, and nations feel bone-deep because they are. We owe much of our humanity to these groups; without their guidance and structure, we could not be fully human. Our participation in cultural life is not just a matter of giving ourselves a label and going along with a few rituals and characteristic activities. Instead, the way we live defines us as a member of a particular group and identifies us, by contrast with other possibilities in our lives. Because we can become fully human only by living in social groups, our very being is tied to them.

Loyalty and Marriage

When a romantic relationship begins, the bond between the partners is often relatively shallow and is often based primarily on physical attraction. Even when two people are strongly attracted to each other, they recognize that the relationship is relatively fragile in the beginning. Events or interactions that would barely trouble a more well-established couple can destroy a relationship in its early stages because attachment grows gradually. In the early part of a relationship, attachment is like a freshly planted tree whose roots have not yet grown deep enough for it to maintain itself upright in a storm.

Pleasure and Loyalty

A couple's bond is not just a matter of time, of course. We grow attached to our partners by sharing experiences with them. In dating relationships, the individuals strive to make their time together as pleasant and interesting as possible. Sharing positive experiences certainly helps build attachment between partners. Having fun together and enjoying each other's company is an important part of building a strong marriage. As we saw in Chapter Four, most social scientists focus their attention primarily on the way that pleasurable interactions strengthen relationships. One of the clearest ways distressed couples differ from couples who are prospering is that unhappy couples have far fewer pleasurable interactions and do not tend to share enjoyable leisure activities very often. Clearly, the social scientists' assumption that people are essentially pleasure seekers does capture some of our nature, but pleasure is only the most obvious way in which a strong relationship can develop.

Suffering and Loyalty

The emphasis on sharing pleasurable experiences is helpful, and many relationships wither partly because couples find it hard to enjoy themselves together because of pressures related to work and children or because of ongoing conflict. If we limit our understanding of the bond between partners to the enjoyable experiences they share, we will have a very one-dimensional and distorted view of marriage. The superficial focus on seeking pleasure and avoiding pain is one of the chief difficulties of the myth of marital happiness because we cannot fall back on pleasure to support our marriages when we are going through a rough period in our relationships. It is obvious that all of us encounter setbacks, difficulties, and tragedies in our lives. The struggles we experience are an essential part of our lives and our marriages. Many times, the difficulties we encounter affect us deeply by reshaping our lives and changing who we are.

Just as difficult circumstances can change our individual lives, the challenges we face can alter our marriages. Sometimes disruptions and tragedies prove overwhelming to couples. For example, the Miami area was hit by a severe hurricane (named "Andrew") in August 1992. Thousands of people sustained extensive damage to their homes and businesses, and many lost personal items that were priceless to them.

The rebuilding effort lasted six months to a year or longer for many families, and it was extraordinarily difficult because so many people needed to see their insurance agents, hire contractors, and obtain building materials at the same time. In many cases, telephone and electric service were unavailable for weeks or months. You could feel the tension and stress in the air, and people were frequently pushed to the limits of their endurance. It is not surprising that many couples' relationships were strained beyond the breaking point, and they divorced. Many more marriages survived the disaster, and I have encountered a number of spouses who say their difficulties drew them closer.

One of the interesting things about social life in Miami, many years after Andrew, is the frequency with which people still discuss the hurricane and its aftermath. Shortly after I meet someone new the question will come up about how long each of us have lived in

Miami. As soon as we discover that both of us were here in 1992, we almost invariably begin to talk about the hurricane, about where we were when it came, about the damage we incurred, and we swap stories about insurance companies, contractors, and so on. This sharing of trauma was particularly obsessive and lengthy in the years immediately after the hurricane, but such conversations are still animated. Those of us who experienced that disaster feel an almost immediate connection to others who underwent similar travails, and the connection is out of proportion to the amount of time we have known one another.

A similar thing can happen in a marriage: living through a setback or a traumatic event can tremendously strengthen the bond between partners. When spouses experience the "silver lining" of a cloud that has entered their shared life, it is partly because of the way they are handling the problem. If they are able to work together and face the difficulty as a team, the challenges they encounter will strengthen their ties significantly. If the difficulty becomes a wedge that divides them, the tragedy can increase the damage their relationship sustains.

Even if spouses do not manage the stresses particularly well, the mere fact that they have experienced difficulties together can be important. Of course, it is better if partners work on their setbacks together, but simply sharing the experience of job loss, a serious illness, or the death of a loved one can deepen a couple's bond. Partners' attachment to each other can often become deeper through this kind of suffering because the suffering is shared.

Painful experiences make a difference in our lives; they change the way we see ourselves and our world. When you live through a traumatic situation with someone else, it can create a stronger tie because he or she may be the only one who can understand what you have experienced, just as I explained with the bonding between strangers based on their experiences of hurricane Andrew. When you experience serious life stressors with your partner, you may not have to explain yourself to him or her, and you may not even need to say much about your experience at all, because the two of you hold it in common.

For example, my wife and I moved to Miami when our son, Jeremy, was two years old. He had begun talking well before his first birthday, and by the time he was two he was talking nonstop from the moment he woke up to the time he dropped off to sleep. He would often literally fall asleep in midsentence. When we moved, Jeremy began to stutter, and he became very frustrated with this dysfluency. It became clear that we needed to get help for him when he began to put his hand over his mouth and almost stopped talking altogether. Seeing his distress was deeply painful to Susan and me because his speech had been such a joyful, endearing experience, and his silence echoed with defeat and pain. We were very surprised by how strongly our move had affected him.

We consulted a speech therapist, who gave us suggestions for helping him overcome the dysfluency, and we followed her recommendations to help Jeremy recover his speech. Susan and I make frequent references to that period in our lives, and even though it is still a painful memory, it is clear to us that we understand one another without our having to say much about it. This relatively mild difficulty in our lives is one of many sources of the bond we share.

Regular Life and Loyalty

Our attachments grow through positive experiences and shared suffering, but the bonds of marriage also grow as we wend our way through the mundane aspects of our everyday lives. I have seen one of the clearest examples of how everyday experiences can lead to a strong sense of loyalty in the way a friend of mine, Rachel, has discussed her relationship with a colleague in her department in another university.

Rachel has complained frequently about the differences of opinion she has had with Bill, and she has often felt that he does not carry his full weight in completing departmental work. Rachel and

Bill have worked together for over twenty years. They could not be more different in personal style, in the way they want things done in the department, or in the way they teach. They only rarely agree with one another in faculty meetings, and they have never had a friendship outside of work. There was a recent attempt by university administrators to encourage Bill, who is an older faculty member, to retire, which involved some financial incentives. Encouraging retirement through incentives is common in many workplaces, but it was clear that he did not want to retire and the "encouragement" to do so was not always benign. Rachel was quick to defend Bill and to do what she could to curb the zeal for his retirement.

When Rachel stood up for Bill, she did not do so as a close friend, as someone who had shared pleasant experiences with him, or even as a close collaborator who stood to lose someone who had helped her in her work. Rachel said that she simply felt that she and the university owed Bill a certain amount of loyalty for the decades of service he had rendered. I was very taken with Rachel's admirable demonstration of loyalty for someone in whom she did not have a personally vested interest. This loyalty grew through many years of simply working together, even in the absence of a closer personal tie.

It is often difficult to recognize how our attachments in marriage grow, simply as a result of our living together and taking care of the day-to-day business of life. This slow, quiet building of attachment is often obscured by more prominent experiences, positive and negative, but I am convinced that simply sharing our lives adds to the bond we feel with our partners.

For example, a child (a friend of a friend) thought his parents were different from married people in the movies. They didn't say sweet things to each other, and he never saw them kiss. He used to feel unhappy about it until the day the dam broke and their farm was flooded. He was put in the attic for safety, and he lay there in the dark, shivering while the rising water lapped at the foundations of the house. In his fear for himself and his parents, he looked out the attic window. Lightning split the dark, and he saw his parents, up to their thighs in swirling water, walking shoulder to shoulder with their heads down, against the wind. His mother had an armful of frightened chicks she'd rescued from the henhouse. His father was carrying a newborn lamb. He saw them only for a fraction of a second, but he never again worried about whether they acted like loving couples in the movies. He was convinced that they had something far stronger than what he saw in the movies.

Fortunately, the kind of attachment that is born of spouses' working together does not rule out their being affectionate, but the bonds between partners do not depend solely on mutual emotional gratification. The still waters of this couple's attachment ran deeper than the absence of obvious displays of affection would indicate.

Loyalty and Becoming a Spouse

It is easy to see how rewarding experiences can bring partners closer together. How is it that painful and mundane experiences contribute to a couple's attachment? Loyalty between partners grows out of the same sources as loyalty to family, culture, and nation. It begins with identification as a member of a group. When it comes to marriage, this membership is solemnized in a marriage ceremony that publicly proclaims the marital tie. We identify ourselves frequently as married, with our wedding rings and in many other ways. Our marital status is one of the first questions people ask about us as they get to know us. Over time, this bond increases in strength through the many activities that make up married life: sharing a living space, eating together, sleeping together, making love, making joint plans, commingling finances, having children, arranging domestic chores, and ten thousand other activities. In other words, because we act married, we define ourselves as married, and we become spouses. Moreover, others recognize that we are married and interact with us as married people.

Although we usually see ourselves as fairly consistent and stable, there is no permanence to our identities or our lives. Our identities are never completely settled or finalized, because if we change how we act, we are changing who we are. There really is no inner identity that exists separately from how we live and act. Our identity is formed by the choices we make, the way we act, and the life projects we undertake. Of course, each of us is born with a particular temperament and with certain inclinations, but these features do not define us entirely as human beings. Who we are and what our lives amount to can take shape only over time, as we live out our lives. That is why Heidegger refers to life as a "happening," as something that unfolds over time. Our options are drawn, for the most part, from the possibilities our culture offers; thus the identity that we create through our choices and actions is one that others can understand and that can fit into our social world. We make ourselves who we are through choosing and acting on the available alternatives.

We make ourselves into married people on the basis of our ideas about what a spouse is and should be. A person becomes a good husband or a good wife by acting in ways that are considered good. In the same way, someone can become an unfaithful, shrewish, or neglectful spouse by consistently taking on those roles in the marriage. In taking on a particular stance or role in marriage, we are what we make of ourselves in enacting the marriage.

Because marriage is such an important part of life, our identity is strongly shaped by how we orient ourselves to marriage. I have asked dozens of spouses if they thought being married to their partners had made them different people. None even hesitated to say that marriage had changed them. Our entry into marriage, and the innumerable experiences, choices, and interactions we have in our marriages—positive, negative, and mundane—help make us who we are as people. The contributions of marital experiences to our identity, and the sheer weight of the shared history that spouses accumulate through the years, can create a very strong bond and give rise to a powerful sense of loyalty.

If we see our relationships with important others in terms of loyalty, we recognize our identity in them, and we acknowledge the enduring bonds between us and the partiality we feel for them. The concept of loyalty-based attachments stands in stark contrast to behavioral or social exchange theories of marriage. For example, so-cial science theories depict spouses as somewhat disengaged, ratio-nal actors who weigh their relationship options *impartially*. They describe spouses as though we could really be neutral about whether or not we should remain in our marriages, as though the balance of costs and benefits will determine whether we will remain married.

In contrast, the *hallmark* of loyalty, as Fletcher reminds us, is the reluctance to exit a relationship when there are difficulties or when a more attractive alternative beckons. In my experience as well, most spouses who consider divorce do so with a great deal of reluc-tance. Research on divorce clearly demonstrates that for most spouses the decision to end a marriage is frequently extended and difficult, progressing in fits and starts, and accompanied by self-doubt and a very significant sense of loss.[6] Even when a decision to divorce is made quickly, it usually follows an extended period of un-happiness with the marriage, which is brought to an end by some dramatic event, such as an affair. For the vast majority of spouses, then, the question is not whether they are loyal to their spouses but how long a sense of loyalty keeps them in their marriages.

Of course, the reluctance that I am calling "loyalty" could be ex-plained as a "barrier" to divorce, according to social exchange the-ory. The feelings of loss and disorientation that accompany divorce are among the emotional costs of ending a marriage, and at that level the theory seems to work. Yet I am reluctant to accept the idea that people are normally relationship "accountants" who coldly and impartially calculate what is in their individual interest.

The concept of loyalty seems to provide a much better under-standing of the deep, complex bonds that people develop for one another. The presence of loyalty helps us see why some people stay together through long periods when the relationship rewards are few. Loyalty also explains the bonding that often occurs between partners who have suffered together, as well as the ties that develop through a couple's shared endurance of the tragedies that life can bring. Moreover, loyalty helps explain how the everyday acts involved in living and working together over an extended period steadily build a bond between partners. The lens of loyalty offers a much sharper and richer way of seeing the ties that bind us to others than do marital theories based on notions of emotional gratification, partly because the concept of loyalty encompasses more of life in its portrayal of how relationships are strengthened.

Loyalty as a Virtue

So far, I have presented loyalty in terms of an emotional attachment or bond that develops through the experience of a significant shared history. This portrayal is accurate, as far as it goes, but loyalty is more than attachment. It is also a virtue that can be cultivated in ways that strengthen a marriage. The feeling of attachment we have for others is the emotional component of loyalty, but virtues have behavioral and intellectual aspects, too.

The key element of all virtues, including loyalty, is that the virtuous person characteristically acts for the sake of the good. You can exercise the virtue of loyalty only if you go beyond feeling attached to your spouse and act in loyal ways toward your partner. There are many ways partners can show loyalty to each other. One simple way to act loyally is to be partial to your spouse's company and to spend time with him or her. Another demonstration of loyalty is to maintain sexual fidelity. Loyal spouses tend to take their partner's side in a dispute and to support the partner's endeavors. When we act in ways that help our spouses flourish or that honor them, we are acting loyally.

The intellectual aspect of loyalty shows up in our ability to recognize that we have incurred certain obligations and debts to our partner in the course of our shared life. We are more likely to practice the virtue of loyalty when we understand that we owe our spouses gratitude, recognition, and allegiance for the many ways in which they have supported us, worked with us, and stood by us through the years. In the course of our marriages, there are many times when we must choose whether to be kind or callous, supportive or indifferent, giving or self-centered, flexible or rigid with our spouses. At these myriad decision points, reminding ourselves of our allegiance and debts to our spouses can help us make positive choices.

I am not talking here about being kind out of guilt or about offering grudging support. When we really recognize everything that our partners have done for us and all that they mean to us, we gladly practice loyalty. When we truly recognize the extent to which we share our lives with our partners and the many ways our spouses have contributed to who we are, it is far easier to stand by them in difficult situations or in circumstances that involve significant temptations. One way to cultivate loyalty is to recall the history you have shared with your partner—the joys, sorrows, and day-to-day experiences that you have had together. This kind of remembrance helps you recognize what is at stake in your life, what you and your spouse have as a couple, and what you stand to lose if you succumb to inducements to disloyalty.

For example, Stuart, a forty-three-year-old accountant, describes his sense of loyalty in explaining his sexual fidelity to his wife, Cindy. He goes on many business trips each year, and several women on these trips have made their interest in having sexual encounters with him very clear, but he has never taken them up on their offers. When I asked him why, he said, "I just can't do that to Cindy. With all we've been through together and how much she means to me, I couldn't betray her like that. She doesn't deserve to be treated that way."

There are many different ways to build a worthwhile shared life. The ideals that you and your spouse adopt for your marriage define what a good marriage is for you. All three components of the virtue of loyalty—the emotional, the behavioral, and the intellectual—show up when you attempt to bring your ideals to life in your marriage. The emotional attachment you feel to the kind of life you want to live with your partner helps keep you focused on attaining it. You can realize your ideals in your relationship only to the extent that you faithfully act toward those ends over the long haul. You are being loyal when your actions help foster the kind of marriage you value.

One of the most important ways that you can foster your desire to act loyally is to remind yourself of the ideals you share with your spouse and why you believe that is the best way to live. By recognizing what is good and reminding yourself of it, you exercise the intellectual component of virtue. We strengthen our loyalty to our partners and our ideals by feeling, acting, and thinking loyally.

Contracts and Covenants

As we saw in Chapter Three, our society has come to see marriage as a contract between two people, one that can be broken when its terms are not met by one or both of them. Over the past three centuries, the terms of the contract have become more demanding and more focused on emotional satisfaction.

Another important change is the erosion of the idea that marriage is a covenant rather than just a contract. The Bible recounts that Jews became the covenant people by promising to worship God and abide by God's laws, and it was promised to them in turn that they would become God's chosen people. This covenant changed the Jewish people and gave them a new identity—indeed, a singular identity that shaped their lives. In other words, their having entered into a covenant helped to define who they are.

The idea of the covenant comes to us from the Judeo-Christian tradition, but it is not only a religious concept. Abraham Lincoln interpreted the Declaration of Independence as a covenant for Americans, by which we promise to uphold a set of principles that define us as a people. The ideals of freedom, equality, and the pursuit of happiness are at the core of our identity as Americans. They make America unique as a nation. If we did not fulfill our commitment to these ideals, we would lose our identity as Americans.

Covenants are more comprehensive and more binding than contracts, partly because covenants are an essential part of our identity. A contract obligates us to a limited commitment that can be broken with relative ease. A contract is usually time-limited as well. A covenant is a more powerful form of commitment that is not so limited, either in its scope or in its duration. In a covenant relationship, we bind ourselves to an undetermined set of obligations that may go on for our entire lives and involve our entire selves, not just our working hours or financial arrangements. A covenant is comparatively unconditional and difficult to dissolve.

It makes sense to think of marriage as a covenant rather than as a contract. Marriage is a key aspect of our identities, and the longer two people live together, the stronger the bond between their shared life and their identities becomes. You define yourself as a spouse through your marriage vows, and in the course of acting as a spouse. The commitment you make to your spouse is not (or at least should not be) limited to a circumscribed set of obligations, nor is it a time-limited agreement. Marriage vows should count for more than business agreements or mortgage contracts. Marriage involves your entire self, not just limited aspects of your life.

Louisiana and Arizona recently enacted covenant marriage laws, to provide a legal avenue for recognizing a stronger commitment to marriage. When couples marry in these states, they have the choice of a standard marital agreement or a covenant marriage. The covenant marriage includes provisions for premarital counseling and for making divorce more difficult (a waiting period and mandatory marital counseling). At the very least, this creative attempt to strengthen marriage offers couples a choice about the way they want to see their marriages and prompts them to think about the kind of commitment they want to make.

Of course, the law only makes the relationship harder to enter and harder to end. It does not (and should not) define the nature of the covenant itself. In other words, what is missing in the law is what the covenant is for. The Jewish covenant has to do with the monotheistic worship of the true God; the American covenant involves the promotion of democratic freedom. What is a couple's covenant for? Clearly, a covenant relationship must involve more than just two people making each other happy. The specific provisions of your covenant with your spouse are up to you. You decide what kind of marriage you want to create, on the basis of the shared ideals or goals that you are pursuing.

The Limits of Loyalty

It is easy to see that loyalty can be misplaced at times. There are many situations in which it would be foolish to remain loyal to a spouse. When a spouse is abusive, unfaithful, or addicted to alcohol or drugs, a wife or a husband must question the degree and form of his or her loyalty. Deciding how loyal we should be can be difficult at times, even excruciating, because our lives are complex and ambiguous. There are almost always good reasons to exercise loyalty, or to curtail our loyalty; everything depends on how we see the situation. How do we decide?

As we saw in Chapter Six, judgment is a key to exercising virtue. Judgment involves, not criticism or self-righteousness, but reasoned choices about how we should act. When we exercise judgment, we think about what is at stake in a particular situation, and we try to decide how to act so that we do our best to foster the good in the particular circumstances.

For example, you may recognize that you owe your spouse an obligation of loyalty in a situation in which your partner has had an argument with a member of your family. Do you express your loyalty by siding with your spouse? by trying to mediate the conflict? by telling your partner, in a loving and supportive way, where he or she went wrong? Recognizing what is important in a situation informs us about what we should do and guides us in knowing how to exercise the virtues, as well as in knowing which ones to emphasize. There are no fixed rules that can tell us what is important in all circumstances, and so we must make judgments that are based on our best perceptions of what is at stake.

Spouses sometimes have split loyalties. For example, a decision has to be made about whether to take care of a sick parent or help a beleaguered partner, to work late or spend time at home. The appropriate degree of loyalty will vary according to how urgently your help is needed by your parent, your spouse, your company, or your children. It will also depend on how balanced your responses have been to these competing commitments in the past and on any number of other aspects of the situation.

Judgment involves seeking the golden mean between excess and deficiency in our actions, then the virtue of loyalty lies between blind, selfless devotion, on the one hand, and detachment, on the other. Because the degree of loyalty that is appropriate to one situation may be woefully inadequate to another and excessive in a third, judgment comes into play. For example, does loyalty call on you to make your relationship a higher priority than holding to your opinions or desires at a given time? You make this decision on the basis of what you think is most important in the particular situation. Sometimes your individual needs or viewpoints should take priority over relational harmony, as when you feel that you are being treated unfairly or exploited in your marriage. In a marriage characterized by abuse or exploitation, for example, a high degree of loyalty would be ill advised.

The development of a significant relationship and its maintenance over time will require loyalty, both to your partner and to the ideals you share with your spouse. Loyalty sustains your ongoing participation in your marriage, through the difficult times and through the mundane routines of everyday life. Loyalty is necessary in maintaining a marriage over time because feelings of love and happiness ebb and flow, and these emotions are not reliable in sustaining relationships. Loyalty is the stable inclination to remain involved even when the relationship is not rewarding or exciting. Practicing the virtue of loyalty means recognizing that you and your partner have become part of each other, acknowledging that you owe each other a great deal, and acting accordingly.

8

The Virtue of Generosity

Fashioning a Giving Marriage

Familiar acts are beautiful through love.
Percy Bysshe Shelley[1]

One of the difficulties in living with someone for many years, even someone you love very much, is that you are bound to gain intimate knowledge of your partner's faults. No matter how much you love your partner, no matter how strong your friendship, no matter how loyal you are, you cannot help being aware of your spouse's shortcomings, foibles, and inadequacies. Over time, you become so familiar with your spouse's human limitations that it is very much like walking through a furnished room. You learn to make your way around the furniture. Some of the furniture can be moved, of course, and some of it can even be mostly eliminated, but because we are human, there will always be some imperfections.

A colleague told me an anecdote that offers a nice metaphor for coming to terms with our partners' weaknesses. He told me about Jim and Sarah, who had been married for ten years. Jim loved to eat oatmeal for breakfast, and Sarah cooked it for him nearly every morning. Invariably, she would be distracted by making lunches or helping their children get ready for school, and some lumps would form in the cereal. Jim hated lumps. He would complain bitterly that he had been telling Sarah about this for years and that she continued to serve him lumpy oatmeal. Sarah would defend herself and remind Jim of some of his faults. Therefore, most days began with a fight.

I often tell this story and ask people what Jim should do. Some people say he should make his own oatmeal. Others say he should eat something else. My favorite answer is that he should simply learn to eat around the lumps. In this way, he can acknowledge his wife's kindness in making oatmeal for him and still enjoy his breakfast.

In marriage, too, there are always lumps. The question is, can we eat around them? Because we must live with and through our own and our spouses' limitations, lifelong marriages require the virtue of generosity, which can help us see the positive as well as the negative in our partners and our marriages. When you practice generosity, you recognize your partner's faults and the difficulties in your relationship, but you also see these things in the context of the positive. Generosity is the ability to see the best in your partner but also to recognize and forgive the human frailty that is also inevitable. If, in spite of your being generous and accepting, there are far more lumps than oatmeal, then extending yourself further may not make sense. It may be time to exercise courage by confronting these lumps.

In ancient and medieval times, the virtue of generosity or liberality was understood primarily in terms of being openhanded with money or possessions. It was an obligation of the wealthy or the noble to give to one another and to their social inferiors. Over time, the meaning of generosity has changed. We have come to see it as more general, and it refers to any kind of giving. We all recognize that we can be generous with our time or talents, sharing them without necessarily looking for recompense. As a consequence, generosity is now seen as a trait that anyone can cultivate, not just the wealthy or the noble. We may expect more from those who are more fortunate in material wealth, talent, or energy, but even the poorest or least talented can give to others.

Being generous means giving more than is required. Certain obligations are commonly understood to be part of being a spouse—

being faithful, communicating clearly, helping one another, contributing to the household, and so forth. Being generous in a marriage means going beyond what is required and in some way offering more. There is an infinite variety of ways in which you can be generous with your spouse, but I want to highlight three here: acknowledging and appreciating your partner's best qualities, forgiving inevitable failings, and giving care and attention.

Seeing the Best in Each Other

I have learned some profound lessons about generosity from my wife, Susan. I often experience some wonder that she can put up with me. I know that I am not the worst of husbands, but I am very aware of my faults—impatience, irritability, and a tendency to isolate myself—which make it quite a challenge to live with me. Yet Susan continues to love me and remain committed to me. Fortunately for both of us, her attachment to me is not enabled by long-suffering martyrdom alone. She is courageous enough to let me know when I have gone too far or indulged myself in an unreasonable bout of irritability.

Just as I was preparing to write about generosity, Susan let me know that I had been rather grouchy the night before. I knew she was right, and so I contritely agreed and told her I was sorry. Then, because this topic was on my mind, I asked her how she tolerates my off-and-on testiness. She said that she sees past it. She is able to see my faults in the context of what I do well, and that renders them more tolerable and helps her see me as a whole person rather than just a grouch.

But Susan goes farther than that. One of her most endearing traits is that she is not shy about reminding me of the good she sees in me. In my better moments, I can recognize that I do have a few redeeming qualities. At other times, I am so self-critical that I feel I have only faults. But Susan has always been clearly aware of the good in me. The constancy with which she sees the best in me is, in my mind, a profound act of generosity, something for which I am deeply grateful. Susan's willingness to see me in a positive light contributes strongly to the attachment I feel for her. I can't tell you how much her generosity means to me. It is such a wonderful gift that makes me love her as much as anything else about her does. It draws me closer to her and reminds me that this relationship is a good place to be.

Seeing the best in someone else, particularly your spouse, is a priceless gift. It is a gift because you are not required to give it and cannot be forced to do so. It is meaningful only if it is freely and sincerely offered. I am fully aware that Susan does not have to see the best in me, and I could never make her do it. The fact that her generosity is a gift makes it all the more meaningful to me.

Recognizing the best in each other is one of the surest ways to encourage the goodness in each other. There is no better way to inspire people to be their best than recognizing the times when they are at their best. If we express appreciation or admiration for the little favors and helping acts that our spouses often do, we make it much more likely that they will do them again. Acknowledging another's good qualities helps draw that goodness out.

One wonderful aspect of generosity is that even though we are giving a gift to others, the gift comes back to us in many ways. What is more, seeing the best in another is a gift that doesn't even cost us anything. It doesn't cost us a thing to offer a compliment, to smile, or to give a word of encouragement. If you are not used to looking for the positive in your partner, it may take some effort to recognize the good in him or her, but once you get the habit, you will find it easy to maintain. Learning to become generous, like the acquisition of all the other virtues, is a matter of intentional practice.

In my work with distressed couples, I have seen that partners' ability to recognize the good in each other is one of the most effective ways to rebuild a marriage. For one couple, Janet and Bill, the cultivation of generosity was the most important change they made. They came to me in despair about their marriage. They found themselves embroiled in heated conflict with great frequency. They were emotionally exhausted by these running battles, but neither could stop doing the things that drove the other to distraction.

My first priority was to understand their difficulties as clearly as I could. Once that was accomplished, I asked them what they liked about each other. You could have heard a pin drop. At first they seemed to take me for a fool. After all, they had just spent forty minutes telling me many of the things that they disliked about each other. Neither of them offered a single thought about the other's good qualities. Undaunted, I asked them if they thought they had ever recognized anything good about each other. Both of them said that they had, of course, but neither of them was willing to be the first to volunteer anything positive about the other.

Our session was just about over at this point, and so I asked them just to try to notice one good thing about each other every day, no matter how small it was. Before they could protest, I told them that they did not have to tell each other, but that I wanted them to write these positive things down. Both Janet and Bill told me in our next meeting that this assignment had been very difficult but that they had completed it on most days. They were still not ready to openly acknowledge each other's good points, nor would they let me read their lists out loud.

I gave them the assignment again, and it was not so hard the second time. In the meantime, we worked on some communication skills and identified particularly provocative behaviors and verbalizations to avoid. Their conflicts began to lose their intensity very quickly, and, over several months, they reclaimed their feelings of love for and commitment to each other. When we finished therapy, both of them told me that the most important thing they had learned was to look for the positive in each other. It had helped them remember why they loved each other, and it made it hard to treat someone they admired so shabbily. Of course, seeing the best in each other is no panacea, but I have never seen it fail to help when spouses have tried it.

Is "Generosity" Another Word for Positive Reinforcement?

Psychologists have been teaching for decades that giving rewards or positive reinforcements is the best way to encourage desirable behavior. There is no doubt that, generally speaking, when you respond positively to what someone does, he or she will be more likely to do similar things in the future. The reinforcement aspect of seeing the best in your partner may partly explain how this form of generosity works.

There are two reasons why recognizing the best in each other is much more than reinforcement, however. First, the whole idea of using rewards to encourage someone else to behave in a desirable way is rather manipulative. This approach to a relationship emphasizes an exchange of goodies: you give me something I want, and I will give you something you want. Sometimes this kind of exchange is perfectly reasonable and very productive, but I do not think most of us want to build our marriages on bartering with each other for what we want. Few of us want our loved ones to give us care and encouragement only so that we will reciprocate it. Seeing these gifts as nothing more than exchanges cheapens them and makes them into ordinary commodities. Reciprocation is important, of course: if we give and give and our spouses only take, then our continued generosity may be misguided. For most of us, however, our primary motivation of giving to our spouses is that we love them and want the best for them. The reciprocal giving in our relationships grows naturally out of our mutual caring and concern.

Another reason why recognizing the best in each other is much more than reinforcement is that when we acknowledge what is good about someone else, we are not simply encouraging an isolated type of behavior. We are helping to shape her identity and encouraging her to see herself as good person who is inclined to act in worthy ways. As we saw in the Chapter Seven, our identities are not determined at birth, nor do they become permanent and unchanging at any time in our lives. Rather, our sense of who we are is somewhat fluid and can change according to our circumstances, our environment, and our choices. Our identities are essentially a story we tell ourselves that explains who we are and why we are as we are. We do not create these stories all by ourselves, of course. The people with whom we live shape our life stories profoundly. This means that our perceptions of each other are vitally important to how we see ourselves.

Seeing the best in other people involves something of a self-fulfilling prophecy: the more we see the best in each other and respond to the good qualities our partners have, the more our partners will identify with that goodness and express it through virtuous action. Our perceptions of and actions toward our partners are powerful enough to influence their sense of who they are, for better or for worse. This means that seeing your spouse's best features consistently will encourage him or her to identify with those positive traits. The more we see ourselves as good persons, the more likely we are to do positive things. Over time, this pattern can become self-perpetuating. We see each other in positive ways, thereby encouraging desirable behavior, which in turn reinforces the positive perceptions. Once this beneficial pattern is in place, it is relatively easy to maintain.

Is Generosity Different from Positive Illusions?

You may wonder how this kind of generosity is different from the positive illusions mentioned in Chapter One. If we try to see the best in each other, aren't we blinding ourselves to real or potential problems that need our attention?

Emphasizing the positive may be especially problematic in the form of marriage recently popularized as a codependent relationship. In this kind of marriage, one spouse is engaged in ongoing addictive behavior, such as alcoholism or gambling. The other spouse overlooks and minimizes the addictive behavior and makes excuses for it. The second spouse is said to enable the problematic behavior because he or she shields the addict from the natural consequences of the addiction. This makes it easier to continue the addictive behavior. By suggesting that generosity is a helpful character trait, am I encouraging this well-documented pattern? If you focus on your spouse's good points, will you then overlook serious problems? There are two answers to these questions.

First, I want to repeat what my wife said about her own generosity in our marriage: that she is able to live with my faults because she can *see past* them; she didn't say that she *does not recognize* them. If she saw nothing but irritability, she would not be willing to stay around. Being generous does not mean being foolish. It simply means being able to see another in a balanced way, in terms of good points as well as weaknesses. Everyone has both. A marriage is made stronger when the spouses focus primarily on each other's positive points.

Of course, there are times when an emphasis on the positive is not only unwarranted but also downright destructive. If your partner is engaging in seriously self-destructive or abusive behavior, then no amount of goodness can tip the balance in his or her favor. Confronting these kinds of problems and putting a stop to them is essential. There are times when the courage to confront difficulties is called for more than generosity. Remember, there are no hard-and-fast rules for deciding what is best in every circumstance; it always comes down to judgment, as we have seen.

Second, all virtues have two attending vices, which correspond to excess or deficiency. In the case of generosity, a deficiency would be stinginess, and excess would be overindulgence. A stingy spouse is reluctant to acknowledge the good in a partner, perhaps from fear of being put in a one-down position. An overindulgent spouse ignores truly intolerable faults and misdeeds or exaggerates the good in a partner in an unrealistic way. When you recognize that generosity is a middle path between stinginess and overindulgence, you can differentiate it from positive illusions and enabling, both of which tend toward excessive generosity. A clear sign that you are being too generous is a feeling that your partner is taking advantage of your efforts, or that you can never give enough. Unfortunately, I have no simple answer to the question of how much generosity is appropriate to every situation. Each set of circumstances calls on you to act differently. You can decide how generous you should be, or whether to be generous at all, by weighing whether your generosity encourages the best in your spouse or encourages your spouse to take advantage of you. You can also find guidance if you think about whether your generosity in a given situation will help bring about the goals you share with your partner. This, too, is inevitably a matter of judgment.

Forgiveness

An anonymous anecdote illustrates the value of forgiveness in the daily life of a couple. A woman relates the story of visiting friends who had just celebrated their fifty-fourth wedding anniversary. The husband came into the house wearing his work boots and left clods of dirt behind him on the spotless kitchen floor. The visitor, expecting the wife to be upset, said, "His boots certainly do bring the dirt in." "Yes," the wife said with a smile as she got up to get the broom, "but they bring him in, too."

Forgiveness is an essential part of any significant long-term relationship. We are all fallible, and from time to time, whether we intend to or not, we will disappoint, hurt, or annoy our partners. No matter how we try, we simply can't be perfect. Whether an offense is large or small, the spouses' ability to forgive each other is necessary to a strong marriage. If spouses cannot forgive each other for their weaknesses and mistakes, then hurt and disappointment will inevitably accumulate to a destructive level. Forgiveness, in principle, is a relatively simple concept, but it can be very difficult to practice.

Even so, you are not *required* to forgive your spouse. Forgiveness, like seeing your partner's goodness, is a gift that is meaningful only if you give it freely. It is an act of generosity because in forgiving your spouse, you are absolving him or her of blame for hurting you or failing you in some way. Releasing your spouse from guilt and blame can be a deeply generous act.

Benefit of the Doubt

Seeing what your partner does as a mistake or a weakness is a crucial part of forgiveness. It is far easier to forgive a hurtful action if you believe that it was inadvertent. There is usually room for this belief because we can never know the reasons for someone's actions with certainty. We always have to interpret the meaning of one another's behavior. In fact, knowing the reasons for our actions is so difficult that we are sometimes at a loss to explain our own behavior.

Given this uncertainty, it seems wise to give your partner the benefit of the doubt whenever possible. When you feel hurt, look carefully to see if the offense was the result of an honest mistake or a weakness. For most of us, most of the time, our partner's misdeeds are mistakes or a result of imperfections. It can be difficult to see something that hurt us as an error, because when we feel hurt or disappointed it is easier to see our spouse's action or inaction as intentional or mean-spirited.

Of course, there are times when people do hurt us intentionally or spitefully. If there is a pattern of hurtful behavior, without remorse or any significant attempts to change it, then the best interpretation may be that it was intentional or at least thoughtless. In these circumstances, simple forgiveness is probably not appropriate. A pattern of abuse or neglect should not be lightly forgiven, for that is when forgiveness is foolish and indulgent. In these cases, meaningful and observable change in the destructive behavior is necessary before the behavior is forgiven.

Earning Forgiveness

There are times when destructive behavior is best understood as a misguided attempt to resolve some difficulty. Hurtful acts can be part of a genuine effort to develop greater intimacy or teamwork, but these worthwhile goals may be pursued in undesirable ways. For example, with one couple, Bill and Sandy, whom I saw as a therapist, the husband was very controlling and verbally aggressive toward his wife. Bill wanted to know where Sandy was at all times, and he did a great deal to discourage her from spending time apart from him with her friends and family. By all accounts, his behavior toward her was domineering and mean-spirited. Bill and Sandy came to see me because Sandy, fed up with Bill's behavior, had moved out. Nevertheless, they both wanted to work out their problems and renew their marriage.

I worked with Bill to help him understand how his behavior was pushing his wife away. I started with the assumption that Bill wanted something important and worthy, which had become distorted, so that his desire was now being expressed in this negative way. Over the course of a few weeks, Bill was able to acknowledge that his controlling behavior was due to his profound insecurity. His marriage was enormously important to him, but it was very difficult for him to give Sandy credit for her commitment and fidelity. He had learned that people were basically untrustworthy, and he thought (not very consciously) that the only way to keep Sandy involved with him was to prevent her from having much contact with others. He believed that if she spent time with other people, she was bound to leave him because she would discover that they were so much better than he was.

It took several weeks of exploration to clarify his fears, and Bill had to exercise a good deal of courage to recognize his insecurity and admit it to Sandy. After several months of hard work, he was able to learn to trust Sandy. It turned out that he had always had every reason to trust her: she was very loyal to him, even defending him from her family's and friends' irritation with his behavior. It was Bill's lack of faith in himself and in Sandy that had made it hard for him to recognize her loyalty.

Sandy was able to forgive Bill for his mistrust and controlling behavior partly because she believed that his reasons for this controlling behavior grew out of a misguided expression of insecurity and out of his deep attachment to her. Even more important, however, Bill demonstrated that he was willing to stop his controlling behavior, and this made it reasonable for Sandy to give him another chance. Bill learned to trust Sandy, and he worked hard to stop questioning her about where she was from moment to moment. He learned to tell her what he wanted from her rather than criticizing and berating her for failing him.

Even with these heartfelt and hard-won changes, however, it was still understandably difficult for Sandy to forgive Bill, because he had hurt her very deeply, both by controlling her in coercive ways and by groundlessly mistrusting her. She teetered back and forth about whether she could forgive him, but she finally decided to do so because she believed in his good intentions, saw his remorse, and experienced his changed behavior.

It was very clear to me that this forgiveness was a generous act because in many ways it would have been easier for Sandy simply to walk away; she could have felt perfectly justified in doing so. Through months of marital therapy, Bill and Sandy were able to rebuild their marriage on a foundation of trust and mutuality. Forgiveness may not always be the best alternative in such circumstances, but Sandy and Bill showed me how powerful it can be in rebuilding a marriage.

An extramarital affair is another serious transgression in which forgiveness becomes a central issue. The first question, of course, is whether both members of the couple want to work through the affair and rebuild their marriage. If they do want to work on their marriage, the central goal of therapy becomes to make healing possible through forgiveness. In my experience, the spouse who was betrayed needs to be able to express his or her pain and anger about the affair, which often takes an extended period of time. The betrayed partner also needs to know that his or her spouse understands this suffering and accepts responsibility for inflicting it. Once this pain has been expressed and responsibility accepted, the spouse who was unfaithful can ask for forgiveness. The ability to forgive this kind of betrayal also frequently requires the spouses to determine what it was in their relationship that allowed infidelity to occur so that it can be avoided in the future.

I have seen many couples damaged by affairs, and in every case it was very difficult for the betrayed spouse to forgive. Infidelity can inflict a very deep wound because we value sexual fidelity so much. After an affair, the relationship cannot flourish without forgiveness, but forgiveness can only be given freely, and in the betrayed spouse's own time. Sitting for many hours with people who struggled to forgive their unfaithful partners helped convince me that forgiveness is an act of generosity.

Keeping Small Problems Small Through Forgiveness

I have used the extreme examples of abuse and extramarital affairs to talk about forgiveness. Fortunately, most couples do not have to cope with either of these damaging situations—but this doesn't mean that there is not much to forgive. The more ordinary hurts and disappointments in a marriage may not cut so deeply, but they do tend to accumulate and to fester if we can't find some way to come to terms with them. They include a multitude of common sins (squeezing the toothpaste tube in the middle, everyday miscommunications, inattention, and the like). Each is small enough in itself, but if we take even these small problems personally, or if we see them as evidence of our partner's lack of consideration, they will drive an enormous wedge between us and our spouse.

It is essential for us to forgive each other for such momentary lapses, and even for characteristic flaws. This may be the basis of the Jamaican proverb advising us to keep both eyes open before marriage, and to shut one eye afterward. We may be able to go beyond that, by seeing past our spouse's weaknesses and recognizing his or her strengths and goodness. For most of us, this goodness more than compensates for our partner's human fallibility. When we allow ourselves to see our partner's strengths—courage, commitment, fidelity, friendship, and so on—it is usually clear that the goodness outweighs the foibles. Our ability to see the big picture can go a long way toward encouraging us to practice generosity as we confront each other's imperfections.

Forgiveness is also extremely valuable to the partner who forgives. When you forgive, you give away the hurt. It is the only way to move beyond the offense and let go of the negative feelings that accompany it. When you can't forgive, you continue to carry hurt around inside you, which means that you are, in a way, continually victimized by memories of what has happened to you. Forgiveness is often an important element of healing the wounds we all experience in our lives.

It is not always easy to know when to forgive. We can be deficient or excessive in the generosity of our forgiveness, just as with the other virtues. Withholding forgiveness when it is appropriate suggests a smallness of character that restricts the quality of the marriage and encourages grudges and recriminations. By contrast, forgiving our partners when forgiveness is premature or unjustified is overindulgence and may actually encourage undesirable behavior.

When Forgiveness Won't Work

There are some things our partners do that we cannot simply forgive. Some of these things involve big problems, such as infidelity or abuse, which require observable changes and time to work through. Others may be small, persistent habits that we would like to overlook but just can't. When forgiveness seems appropriate, and when you can't manage to forgive even though you have genuinely tried, this is a message that something important about the problem needs more attention. If you are not ready to forgive, it may be important for you, together with your partner, to confront the problem more fully or more directly.

In situations where forgiveness is difficult, it may be important to find the courage to confront the problem and work it out together. Sometimes hurt and misunderstandings are more than spouses can handle on their own, and the assistance of a professional therapist can help. It can be difficult at times for spouses to know whether they should forgive their partners; talking about the situation with a professional may clarify how the problem can be resolved. Nevertheless, some injuries are beyond a person's capacity to forgive, and sometimes a marriage is so irreparably damaged that divorce becomes the only reasonable alternative.

The best kind of outcome when one spouse hurts or disappoints the other is for the offending spouse to come to understand what was hurtful or disappointing, ask for and receive forgiveness, and then avoid a repetition of the incident. The worst kind of situation occurs when the offense is too grievous or persistent to allow forgiveness and the couple cannot remain together. Of course, many situations are in between these extremes, and forgiving our spouses may involve coming to terms with their weaknesses without reaching the complete resolution we prefer. In these instances, we may decide to forgive our partners but also recognize that we have to protect ourselves in some way so that our spouses do not let us down in the same way again. The key to this kind of forgiveness is to recognize the limitations that led our partner to injure us and to take steps to minimize the impact that such weaknesses have on us and our marriages.

This approach to forgiveness does not necessarily mean that we absolve our partners from all responsibility for hurting us. It only means that we understand why they did what they have done, and that we recognize how their human flaws made it difficult for them to do better. If an injury is so deep that we cannot tolerate the chance of its happening again, then we need to take steps to protect ourselves. In this situation, the same recognition of limitations that allows us to forgive also means that we should not allow ourselves to be vulnerable to those flaws again. When we know that someone has a weakness that is difficult for him or her to change, and when we want to maintain the relationship, we have to learn to work around the weakness.

For example, Linda and Ken began their marriage by pooling their finances, using a joint checking account, and sharing credit cards. It did not take long for Linda to see that Ken was spending more money than they had. With maddening frequency, he would use their credit cards until he reached their credit limit, and he would write checks that they could not cover. Linda herself was very responsible with money, and she was humiliated when she had to deal with bounced checks or discovered that she could not use her credit card because the limit had been reached. Linda would confront Ken, and he would promise to do better, but he was unable to be more responsible with money.

Linda loved Ken very much, and in many ways he was a very good husband and father. After many arguments, Linda finally told Ken that he had to give her the entire management of their finances. She would give him cash, which he could spend, and she would pay the bills and manage the checking account and credit cards. Ken agreed because he could see the problems he had created.

Linda had learned that Ken could not use checks and credit cards responsibly. She was able to forgive him for this shortcoming, but only by arranging things so that his weakness in this area did not continue to create problems for them. Ken made it easier for Linda to forgive him by accepting responsibility for his weakness and by honoring their new financial arrangement.

Giving of Ourselves

There are also smaller, more common, but no less important ways in which we can give to each other. A third form of generosity is to give of ourselves. This kind of giving can take myriad forms, from small kindnesses, such as catering to each other's preferences and listening to each other, to larger ones, such as offering support and encouragement when a spouse has experienced a significant defeat or a loss. Offering both the small and the great gifts of self contributes a great deal toward building a strong marriage.

In the midst of our busy lives, simply listening to each other attentively is an act of generosity, for there are always many things vying for our attention. Trainers in communication skills correctly stress the importance of learning to listen as a way of enhancing a relationship. They talk about listening as a skill, but I think it is better understood as a form of generosity. All you have to do is think about—or, better yet, practice—listening to your spouse for three to five minutes, without bringing in any of your own concerns or allowing yourself to be distracted by other things. Just try to pay close attention to what your partner is saying and encourage him or her to go on talking. It is easy to see that this is a gift of self. Giving it on a regular basis can be very enriching to a marriage.

Offering compassion for your spouse's suffering can be another very important form of giving. For example, I am a university professor, and a few years ago, when I was going through the infamous publish-or-perish experience, my wife's compassion was a lifeline. I had worked very hard and done well enough that my immediate supervisors enthusiastically encouraged me to apply early for tenure rather than wait out the customary six-year probationary period. But the people at higher levels who reviewed my application turned me down. They encouraged me to reapply the next year. Simple.

The denial of tenure was the single most disappointing and painful experience I have ever had. It devastated me. I had devoted myself to that goal for many years and worked unceasingly to build a scholarly record. I also felt deeply humiliated because a decision on tenure is very public and it was excruciating for me to face people who knew that I had come up short in this crucial evaluation. I felt very fortunate that my family, friends, and colleagues were genuinely supportive and compassionate about this painful setback.

More than anyone else, Susan had a deep understanding of how important tenure was to me, and she felt tremendously hurt as well: she had given of herself by encouraging and supporting me through the successes and discouragements I had already experienced in my career. In many ways my getting tenure had been a joint project for us. My misery gradually decreased, but it was not much fun to be with me for many months. Susan easily could have become impatient with me, in the belief that I should just get over this disappointment and move on. She could have berated me for my self-pity or been disgusted at the bitterness I felt. But she didn't. Instead, she acted generously by treating me with compassion and patience.

The story has a happy ending in two ways. The following year I was granted tenure as though there had never been any real question about it. And through this experience I came to value Susan more than ever before. The gifts of her kindness and devotion and the fact that we had suffered through this painful setback together significantly deepened our bonds of affection and attachment.

Generosity may come easier to some than to others, but it is a virtue well worth cultivating. It can help us see the best in our spouses, without having to rely on positive illusions that help us feel good but can be shattered with relative ease. Unfortunately, however, in recent decades generosity has acquired a bad name in our individualistic society, and it is easy to feel foolish when we are being generous. Clearly, there are times when it is not wise to give of ourselves, but this fact should not lead us to think that generosity is always ill advised. I think it is indispensable to building a strong marriage. As we see the best in each other, encourage each another's goodness, forgive each other, and give of ourselves, we renew our commitment to each other and build stronger bonds.

9

The Virtue of Justice
Fostering a Fair Marriage

*In any common attempt to achieve the good, all gen-
uine collaborators benefit from the contribution of the
others. They are in a sense all in each other's debt.*

Charles Taylor[1]

One of the most important changes in the history of marriage is
the emerging importance of equality between husbands and
wives. Our ideas about what is just in marriage have changed enormously in the past five hundred years. During much of our history,
husbands' control over their wives was so complete that women
were frequently treated as if they were their husbands' property. For
centuries, wives could not hold property themselves, as husbands
even held their wives' inheritances.

Husbands had a right to punish their wives physically for any
challenge to their authority or for any perceived faults, as long as
the beating did not become "excessive." The expression "rule of
thumb" comes from the recognized standard that a husband should
not beat his wife with a stick wider than his thumb. The right to
"chastise" one's wife was justified by the fact that husbands were
held accountable for their wives and children. It has only recently
become a crime for a husband to assault his wife or to force her to
have sex with him.

For centuries, women had little choice but to submit to this arrangement because the only real alternatives to being married were living in a convent, working in some form of domestic service, or becoming a prostitute. Women who deserted or were deserted by their husbands frequently faced economic and social destitution.

Justice Between Husbands and Wives

Rolling back these injustices to make the full benefits of individual rights and personal dignity available to women has been a long, slow process that is not complete even today. It has been a wrenching cultural shift that often leaves men and women alike confused about just what to expect from each other. The contours of fairness between men and women are very poorly defined at this time, and couples are often forced to grope their way toward arrangements with which they can live.

Although very few people call themselves feminists, virtually all of us have been powerfully influenced by the feminists' clarion call for equity between men and women. We have become sensitized to the ways that women are treated unjustly in families. This remarkable change in our ideas about marriage is so widespread that the vast majority of spouses say that they are committed to equity in marriage. Of course, many of us are better at saying we want fairness in marriage than actually working to make our marriages just.

The idea of gender equity has proven compelling to us partly because, in the last two centuries, we have come to see individual rights, dignity, and equality as natural aspects of being human. The possession of individual rights was originally claimed only for propertied men, but human rights and dignity have been steadily expanded to include everyone, at least in principle. In spite of a good deal of opposition, women have been increasingly accorded individual rights and equality.

In addition, gender equity has become important because it is necessary to the affection and intimacy between husbands and wives that we have come to value over the last three centuries. The full measure of intimacy in marriage requires husbands and wives to be equals. Intimacy between husbands and wives is limited when there is a clear difference in power between them, because maintaining control requires the more powerful partner to stand apart from his or her spouse. You cannot share your vulnerabilities and secrets with your spouse if you want to have more power than your partner does. Intimacy between spouses requires a certain degree of fairness in marriage. Frequent experiences of injustice will make it difficult if not impossible for spouses to maintain the kind of trust necessary to clear communication and emotional closeness. How can we best understand and cultivate the justice that has become so important to modern marriage?

Individual Justice

If you are like most people, when you think about justice you see it in terms of providing equal opportunities for everyone and having rules or procedures to make sure that everyone is treated fairly. This is the standard way for contemporary Americans to understand justice. We favor equal opportunities so that everyone will have the chance to seek his or her own happiness and prosperity in life. The legal procedures that protect our individual rights should be applied to everyone in the same way, to maintain our equality. Moreover, these procedures are designed to be neutral about what is good or desirable so that we can all decide how we want to live. You can see that this procedural version of justice fits very well with individualism because it supports the freedom and equality of separate individuals.

Procedural justice is designed for a social world that is made up of separate individuals who make independent and competing claims to money, position, or privilege. People are frequently portrayed as adversaries in dividing up the available burdens and benefits in a society. Separate individuals must defend their prerogatives from one another and from the group. Individuals are the ultimate beneficiaries of appeals to equality and impartial procedures. We accept inequalities in possessions or status as long as we believe that they are due to differences in talent, effort, or fortune. Even though inequalities exist, the key feature of this approach to justice is that it should operate impersonally and in the same way for everyone.

People who promote justice in marriage generally adopt this individually oriented approach to fairness. For the most part, our collective effort to improve marriage by fashioning equality between spouses has been very positive. It has shown us how to combat the injustice that was so prominent in our history and is still present, to some degree, in today's marriages. Equality and impartiality have become increasingly common in marriage. For example, most couples want each partner to have an equal say in important decisions about having children, making major purchases, or finding a place to live. Yet if we focus only on an equal division between partners, we may lose sight of what unites us in marriage, as the following example illustrates.

Millie and Tom came to our training clinic because they were embroiled in endless arguments about fairness in their marriage. They had taken the idea of equality to an extreme because both of them were very concerned about injustice. They went to great lengths to ensure that each took on the same amount of work and received an equal portion of the benefits of their relationship. Thus Millie and Tom scrupulously divided child care time between themselves. They split the household chores as evenly as possible, and they kept their finances separate. They went so far as to divide the grocery bill according to the portion of the groceries that they both used, the portion that Tom used himself, and the portion that Millie wanted. Each paid for his or her portion of the groceries. Unfortunately, however, their extraordinary efforts had not resulted in a shared sense of justice in their marriage. Instead, their emphasis on absolute equality led to interminable disagreements rather than to the just arrangement that they were attempting to create.

Millie and Tom were acting as though they really were independent individuals who were adversaries in an endless round of competitive divisions of household tasks, money, and free time. In the feverish attempts they made to avoid having either one get the short end of the arrangement, they could not see each other as partners who were working together.

Their therapy focused on helping them move from being a pair of competing individuals to sharing a life that united them more than it divided them. They were gradually able to relax their vigilance about injustice as they learned to trust each other and come to terms with their experiences of unfairness in their family histories. With time and effort, they learned that they were both interested in their mutual well-being and happiness. The most important change in their relationship was their learning how to be *partners* so that they could share the work and joys of their marriage instead of fighting over how chores and expenses would be divided.

Inequality and Justice

Few couples would go to the extremes that Millie and Tom did, but an exclusive emphasis on equality in marriage can lead to this kind of grocery-list justice. Even if we think of marital justice as a balance of give-and-take over time, we are still prone to think of fairness in individual terms, as a kind of justice that divides spouses rather than uniting them.

Strict equality between husbands and wives is difficult if not impossible to practice on a day-to-day basis. The differences in spouses' abilities and inclinations lead the spouses to take on different tasks and go about them in different ways. Spouses who have confidence in the fairness of their arrangements generally perceive justice in their relationships in a global way and do not need to struggle over their equality on a daily basis. Over time, and in the main, each partner takes on his or her fair share of the tasks of marriage, and both share their joint resources equitably. Equality may not show up in a given task (child care, paid employment), or it may not be apparent during a particular period of time, but, on the whole, the partners see their relationship as fair. The prominent family therapist Ivan Boszormenyi-Nagy points out that marital partners and other family members come to see each other as trustworthy largely through experiencing this kind of dynamic balance of fairness over time.[2]

There is another reason why the impersonal approach to fairness through social equality and legal procedures is not sufficient for marriage: the abstract idea of a simple, impartial division of tasks and goods between husband and wife is just too cold and calculating. As we saw with loyalty, impartiality is not a useful way to think about the bonds we have in our marriages. We are always partial to those we love, and in loving our spouses and living with them, we come to know their strengths and weaknesses. Indeed, **mature intimacy largely consists in being able to recognize and understand your partner's foibles and admire what is genuinely good about him or her.** Justice in marriage means being able to recognize your own and your spouse's particular capabilities and limitations and arrange your marriage so that these inequalities contribute to your relationship rather than create discord between you.

For example, in one couple I know, Sandy needs more sleep than Jim (her husband) does. Sandy tried for many years to keep the same hours Jim did, but it was damaging to her physical and mental health. They both recognize her need for more rest, and they try to make provisions for Sandy to go to bed earlier and take naps when she needs them. On many occasions, Jim will do some housework or take care of the children while Sandy sleeps. If we look at their marriage in terms of strict equality, this is an injustice because Jim works longer hours than Sandy does, and she sometimes gets to sleep while he works (although sometimes he just goofs off while she rests). Neither Jim nor Sandy sees this inequality as unfair, however, because both of them believe that they are each doing their best to take care of their family. Each is contributing as he or she is best able to do instead of expecting that both of them will do the same amount of work at all times.

Flexible Justice

In my many conversations with couples as a researcher and as a therapist, I have encountered very few spouses who expect a strictly equal division of effort and reward. Instead, husbands and wives understand that each of them will contribute to their marriages in different ways and in differing degrees and that this balance will fluctuate over time. Most spouses see fairness in this dynamic way, and all they usually ask of one another is that each of them do their best to take care of the marriage and the family. Partners learn to trust that each of them will do his or her part to make their shared life what they want it to be. This trustworthiness is one of the key features of a partnership marriage. Husbands and wives come to rely on each other implicitly. They do not need to attend to whether they are dividing the work and benefits of their marriages equally, because they believe they are both committed to doing their best and to sharing the fruits of their lives with each other.

This idea of justice through unity is very different from the individualistic view of justice we find in social exchange theory (see Chapter Four). That popular theory portrays spouses as being preoccupied with counting up the costs and benefits of their relationships. In fact, it is often a clear sign that there is trouble in a marriage when partners begin to tally who does what and who owes what to whom. It signals a breakdown in the trustworthiness that is so important to partnership. Fortunately, questions about our partners' trustworthiness are usually temporary and circumscribed. When spouses feel that they need to compare each other's contributions to the marriage in an ongoing way, it may represent a serious split in their unity.

It is interesting that almost all spouses say they want to share the tasks and benefits of marriage in a roughly equal way, for there is often a clear imbalance in the number of hours that the two spouses work. In most couples, women do the majority of the housework and child care, even when they work as many hours outside the home as their husbands do. This imbalance is distressing to many wives, and they understandably want their husbands to shoulder a more equitable portion of the household work. Women who are employed full-time are twice as likely to see their marriages as troubled if they think the division of household labor is unfair.[3] Yet I have been surprised to hear many women in this situation say that although they would like their husbands to do more, they would be content if their husbands would simply acknowledge the imbalance with gratitude. In other words, one way (although not the best way) to redress an imbalance in the burdens of the marriage is for husbands to acknowledge their wives' efforts. A partner who is doing more than the other is doing deserves more credit, and recognition of these extra efforts is one kind of recompense for them in marriage.

Other couples have arrangements whereby the husband has a very demanding business or professional job and the wife is a homemaker. In recent years, some couples have found it better to reverse this pattern by relying on the wife's employment, with the husband taking care of the home. In most single-earner households the breadwinners are the men, many of whom bear a greater burden because of longer working hours, extensive travel, or the emotionally draining nature of their work. Typically, these husbands are not saying they want their wives to work as hard as they do. Instead, they often want their extraordinarily hard work acknowledged by everyday kindnesses and by their wives' reliable management of many details of married life.

When it comes to sharing the goods of the marriage, whether financial or emotional, a similar understanding is generally present in a strong marriage. Most of us believe that the benefits of marriage should be roughly balanced between husbands and wives, just as the burdens should be. Inequalities are common, of course, and an unequal distribution of goods may not necessarily be unjust.

For example, even though Barbara and Peter each need a wardrobe for work, Barbara has a high-visibility job for which she needs expensive clothing, whereas Peter is a computer programmer and can dress casually. Spending more on her professional wardrobe creates an inequality, but that doesn't create a problem for them. Similarly, Beth and James have very different hobbies. Beth enjoys needlepoint and other crafts, whereas James is an avid music fan who has a very expensive stereo system and a large collection of compact discs. The costs of the two hobbies are vastly different, but this inequality does not trouble them because neither of them senses that James is taking advantage by pursuing his more expensive hobby. In addition, both of them enjoy the beautiful things that Beth creates, and both feel that James's music adds a great deal to the atmosphere of their home.

Confronting Injustice

Although many inequalities seem just, partners in a marriage need to be able to recognize and respond to inequalities that signal injustice. It is important to be able to recognize and confront injustice in marriage, as when one spouse insists on spending a greater share of the couple's money, demands a stronger voice in the couple's decisions, or coerces the other into catering to his or her emotional wishes.

Keri, for example, had come to recognize that her husband, Dan, was treating her unfairly, and she had decided to divorce him unless he could change. He was frequently critical of her, and she felt that she could not do anything right. When they came to me for marital therapy, Keri presented her unhappiness in a very timid, halting way. Dan, true to form, disagreed with her, corrected her, and justified himself at her expense. Keri was relatively easily silenced, but her rage was apparent without her saying a word.

I questioned Dan about his way of interacting with Keri and about what prompted him to be so critical of her. He related several stories about how he had learned valuable lessons when his father had corrected him. As we explored this family pattern of criticism, Dan's initial gratitude for his father's suggestions became mixed with a significant degree of pain, which was due to his feeling that his father had frequently been unfair to him. When I pointed out the similarity of the criticism he had received from his father and the criticism he gave to Keri, Dan went pale. The recognition that he was hurting her in the same way his father had hurt him devastated him. When he saw the injustice of his critical attitude, he immediately began to curtail his negativity. It had taken Keri a long time to build up the courage it took to confront Dan, and it was important for her to learn to speak up for herself and let him know when he was hurting her feelings. She continued to develop her courage, and the change in Dan's stance toward her encouraged Keri to speak to him more directly and clearly.

Unfortunately, injustice in couples is not always so easily remedied. Most of us like to think of ourselves as fair, however, and when we see that we are not being just to our partners, we are often open to change. When fairness is lacking in a marriage, it often reflects the inequalities between women and men in our society. For this reason, we cannot afford to relax our attention to injustice as a matter of gender. The hard-won progress we have made in seeing men and women as equals remains partial. It is still too easy to assume that household chores and child care are primarily women's work, and it is too common to see men as unresponsive bumblers in family life. Sometimes seeing how we have been influenced by cultural patterns that place women at a disadvantage can help us gain some distance from these attitudes and change them more easily because we can see that these inequalities are not just a personal matter between us as partners.

At the same time, our usual way of approaching justice—as an equal distribution of benefits and burdens, managed through impersonal procedures—is insufficient because modern marriage is a very personal relationship, and acceptable inequalities are bound to arise. In addition, if we pay attention only to husbands and wives as equal *individuals*, we will neglect the ways in which spouses can be equal *partners* in a common endeavor. We need to supplement our attention to fairness for individuals with an awareness of how justice relates to the couple as a partnership.

Partnership and Justice

In our individualistic society, it can be hard for us to see how justice might include consideration for social entities (couples, families, communities, nations) rather than only for individuals. If we focus on justice solely in terms of an equal distribution of burdens and benefits between individuals, we will also neglect the care and cultivation of these social entities. The emphasis on splitting things equally between individuals is inherently divisive because it creates an adversarial relationship in which individuals are focused primarily on ensuring that they get their fair share. **But the more we portray fairness as an equal division between individuals, the more difficult it is for us to see how spouses' joint participation in the work and joys of a shared life helps strengthen their marriage.**

We can see the difference between an individual approach to justice and a partnership approach by attending to how we use the word *share*. If we focus on dividing the benefits and burdens of marriage between the spouses, we say that each should have his or her "fair share." A share, in this understanding, is a noun that means a portion: something the individual can possess and that is divided between individuals. The idea that the goods in life are, for the most part, things that individuals possess or experience is central to individualism. By contrast, I have been using the term *share* as a verb, as in "sharing the tasks and goods of marriage," and I have been emphasizing how partners live a "shared life." Here, the term *share* emphasizes the unity of the partners in shouldering the work of the marriage together and experiencing its joys as a couple.

Couples in strong marriages always have an idea of justice that is richer than the formal, abstract ideal of equality between spouses.

These couples recognize the ways in which they are participating in the shared projects that define a marriage as a partnership. The justice they experience unites them because doing their part to further these projects and enjoying the fruits of their joint efforts brings them together. Let's explore how we can formulate a more vibrant understanding of justice in marriage.

Sheri and Bob, whom we met in Chapter Six, illustrate how shared projects create a context for justice in their financial arrangements. Both of them work, Bob as a professor and Sheri as a physical therapist, and they have arranged their work schedules around caring for their children. Bob earns somewhat more than Sheri does, but they pool their income and have agreed on several financial goals. Their financial aims are modest, focused on maintaining a pleasant family life and on the long-term goals of paying for their house, saving for their children's college education, and saving for their retirement. They have agreed on these goals, and they pay no attention to whether each contributes an equal amount of income to their aims. Sheri and Bob will enjoy the fruits of their efforts together as joint owners of their house, they will spend their retirement together, and their children's education will be a mutual achievement.

There is nothing very profound in this simple, everyday example of the way in which many couples pool their economic resources, and yet it illustrates how economic justice in a marriage is often guided more by the partners' shared goals than by how they divide things up. Their financial aims unify them, and fairness is ensured, not by rules for equality, but by their mutual trust that they are both contributing as best they can to the achievement of their purposes. Justice in marriage takes on a very different appearance when we see it in terms of mutual goals and joint effort rather than in terms of dividing burdens and benefits. Justice as fairness between individuals does not really capture the rich form of justice that is possible only in a shared life.

Justice in a Community

Aristotle[4] teaches that justice is best pursued among people who are united by shared goals. In fact, he believes that true justice can exist only in a particular kind of community, called the *polis*, a city-state like the Athens of his time. For him, the *polis* is the center of individual life, and it provides a compact, all-encompassing context within which a person can pursue the good life. Justice, for Aristotle, was to be found only in the context of the shared goals of a particular *polis* because justice is partly defined by the guiding ideals of a given community. For example, equal opportunity to obtain goods (such as political office or wealth) is favored in a democratic community, whereas in an oligarchy (government by the elite) access to these goods is restricted to those who are privileged by birth or wealth. The people who live in each kind of community would defend its distribution of goods as just because these arrangements are consistent with the community's ideals. In other words, what we consider fair depends on what we value and on the social arrangements we see as right.

One of Aristotle's key ideas about the good life is that the most important goods can be held only in common and that the good life is to be found in friendship and in the creation of the best community. Moreover, he believes that people can really flourish only in a well-ordered community, among friends who are devoted to the good of the community and to each other's good. Democracy works only when it is held as a common value; there can be no individual democracy. In the same way, we as a nation and as communities must uphold all our important freedoms if any of us is to securely enjoy them.

Crucial goods like solidarity, harmony, or intimacy are indivisible: they can only be shared, and if we try to divide them up as individual possessions, they disappear. In contemporary society, however, we often see the primary goods in life in terms of money, position, and privilege—in terms, that is, of divisible goods. These are possessions of individuals. The more of them that one person has, the less that other people can have. In our society, we think of democracy and justice as the social frameworks that allow each individual an opportunity to acquire these divisible goods. For Aristotle, however, it is just the opposite. He sees money and status as tools that are necessary to the creation of a good community, but he does not see them as the goals of life.

For better or worse, we do not live in the kind of society that Aristotle describes. Even though we do not live in anything like Aristotle's *polis*, our world remains intensely social. Because most of us live in cosmopolitan cities and our society is highly pluralistic, there is relatively little agreement about how to live the best kind of life. That is why our society has developed the procedural approach to justice. This approach to justice focuses on designing rules that allow all individuals to choose how they want to live. The rules protect each individual's right to pursue his or her own kind of happiness, and, at least in principle, everyone is supposed to be treated equally.

One negative consequence of individualism, however, is that this way of seeing ourselves hides our social ties from us and makes us think we are more separate than we are. When we recognize our dependency on one another for indispensable, indivisible goods, however, we see that well-ordered marriages, families, communities, and nations are collective achievements that make it possible for their individual participants to flourish.

Once we recognize how much of the good life we hold in common, a whole new vista of mutual ties is illuminated for us. We can see that whenever anyone does something that helps to improve the community, everyone in the community benefits. We see that our mutual gratitude and acknowledgment are fitting because we can have a good community only to the extent that all of us support it and work toward making it what we want. Because we depend on one another for the quality of our shared life, we also share an obligation to work toward making our community a good place to live and a place of which we can be proud. By the same token, we are mutually indebted to each other for the ways in which each of us contributes to that good. We are entirely dependent on one another to create the kind of community that will allow us to prosper as individuals. Our fragmented community life is regrettable and sorely in need of remedy, and there is little doubt that a richer communal life would help strengthen marriages.[5]

The Minicommunity of Marriage

We do not live wholly within the cohesive kind of community that Aristotle describes, but we may experience committed communities in our families, churches, synagogues, or civic groups. Marriage can be a kind of minicommunity in which the partners reach substantial agreement about how they want to live. In fact, the partnership marriage described in this book is just such a minicommunity, guided by shared goals and sustained by virtue. Marriage and the family are among the last places in our society where a rich ideal of community survives as a desirable way to live. The idea that marriage is built on the partners' mutual commitment and that it provides a sense of belonging and purpose is well worth preserving. Although the prevalence of the individualistic ethic in our society undermines our ability to maintain the ideal of a minicommunity in marriage, the effort to do so is well rewarded by the solidarity and purposeful kind of life that a partnership marriage makes possible.

It is easy to see that marriage at its best is a communal endeavor. As we create a shared life with our partners, we hold a great deal in common. We can have goods like intimacy, togetherness, belonging, and mutual goals only if we share them. Spouses' common practices of pooling their finances, living in the same dwelling, going places together, and making decisions together make it clear that our lives as married people are profoundly intertwined with those of our partners. As we saw in Chapter Seven, the loyalty we feel toward our families, our children, and our partners differs from what we feel in other relationships and can be extraordinarily deep. Our participation in our marriages even helps shape our identities as individuals. Understanding and cultivating the many sources of solidarity with our partners can help us practice a rich form of justice in our marriages.

One of the most important aspects of a partnership marriage, as of a true community, is that the participants have shared goals. Partnership marriages, like communities, define themselves by the projects that they undertake (raising children, engaging in public service, furthering education, taking part in religious observances) and by the ideals that guide them. Mutual goals and projects set the context for justice in a marriage as in a community. It is virtually impossible to decide what is fair in a partnership marriage without knowing what the couple's goals are.

Decisions about shared goals come before questions of fairness in a marriage; the combination of the partners' goals and the partners' situation defines what needs to be done and how it can be accomplished fairly. For example, let's say a couple is in a canoe on a lake, and both spouses are putting equal effort into the work of paddling. Their effort is worth their time only if they have the same goal and are working together to get there. If one of them wants to paddle directly across the lake and the other wants to cruise around the shore, they will not get anywhere, because they will be at cross-purposes. Even if both of them are paddling with equal vigor, it is nonsense to say that the work of paddling is being distributed fairly unless they are paddling toward the same destination. There is no context for questions of justice if the partners do not have the same goal.

If our canoeists have not yet decided where they are going, however, then they may be appropriately concerned about fairness in choosing their goal. A fair decision can be made in many different ways, of course. The partners may compromise by going directly across the lake and then paddling back along the shore, or they may decide that going around the lake is more important to one of them than crossing it is to the other, and so on. The important thing is that they reach a joint decision to which both can gladly contribute their energies.

Let's take the analogy a step farther and say that the partners have to paddle through an area of the lake where a river enters and creates a current. In this area, the person in the bow has to paddle hard, whereas the person in the stern has the role of steering, a task that requires less effort but more skill. They can get through this area of the lake and reach their goal only if each of them plays his or her part and if they both accept that one of them will be paddling harder than the other.

Justice as a Virtue

The virtue of justice requires more than the creation of a fair distribution of burdens and benefits. For example, we may be acting in ways that bring about fairness merely in order to avoid criticism, or because we think our actions will pay off for us, but primarily self-serving actions are not virtuous. In the practice of justice, as in the practice of other virtues, the right thing must be done for the right reason. Acting justly is virtuous when we do it because we care about fairness, and when our lives are generally characterized by an interest in justice.

For the virtuous person, acting fairly with his or her partner is not a burden or a sacrifice. Becoming characteristically just means wanting to give your partner and your marriage their due. As in the practice of other virtues, acting justly with your spouse becomes second nature as you cultivate your understanding and love of fairness. The goals that you and your partner share will also contribute to your desire to treat each other fairly because injustice makes it more difficult for you to work together on common projects.

Two Dimensions of Justice

When we think about justice in marriage, neither the impartial, procedural model nor Aristotle's approach seems to give us a fully adequate and fitting way to promote fairness. As we have seen, a simple model of equality cannot work because married life is just not simple. An impartial, rule-oriented approach to fairness does not make sense in a highly personal relationship that is, at its best, devoted to shared ideals and purposes. Aristotle's views are helpful with the complexity of justice, but his approach is not adequate either. Although it is helpful to see marriage as a minicommunity, Aristotle does not help us deal with the questions of justice between men and women that have become so important to us.

I believe that justice requires us to seek a balance between the individual interests of the spouses and the shared goals that help define fairness in a marriage. If we try to do without fairness to individuals, we risk falling back into the unacceptably unjust arrangement between husbands and wives that has characterized our history. If we neglect the way that justice is tied to partnership and shared goals, we undermine the bonds between partners, reduce our ability to work together as partners, and neglect the way that marriage is, at its best, a shared life devoted to goods the partners hold in common.

I think the best way to seek a balance between individual interests and partnership is to think about justice in two dimensions. One dimension (the dimension of equality) deals with equality and inequality between the spouses as individuals. The other (the dimension of community) involves the degree to which the spouses focus on their separateness and togetherness.

Equality and Justice

Women have been treated unequally throughout our history, and this pattern of inequity is far too easy to follow if we are not aware of it. Aristotle's idea about virtue as the mean between deficiency and excess can help us avoid taking equality to an extreme. It is easy to see that when someone does not pay enough attention to equality in his or her marriage, he or she is showing a deficiency of justice on this dimension. Individuals who characteristically disregard equality in order to satisfy their individual desires at the expense of their spouses exhibit the vice or character flaw of injustice.

Excessive attention to equality shows up in a partner's insistence on absolute sameness in the benefits and burdens of marriage. We have seen that marriage is full of inequalities in abilities, inclinations, needs, and effort. There are always differences between spouses, and if these differences are acknowledged and used constructively, they are a source of strength. If a spouse insists on everything being made equal, he or she is acting as if these differences did not exist. Even something as admirable as equality can become problematic if it is pushed too far. Many couples find the golden mean by recognizing and accepting some inequalities in ability, interests, and needs, on the one hand, and by seeking equality in trusting their partners to look out for their interests, on the other hand.

Community and Justice

If we accept the cultural priority of the individual and look out only for ourselves as individuals in our marriages, then the only thing that will keep us in our marriages will be individual benefits. A spouse who characteristically focuses only on the benefits of marriage for himself or herself is showing a deficiency of justice with respect to the minicommunity of the marriage. If we attend only to what we receive from marriage, then we are unlikely to give to our marriages in ways that nurture the solidarity and partnership needed for a lifelong relationship.

It is also possible to overemphasize the marriage as a unit and neglect our needs or desires as individuals. This excess of attention to the marriage as a minicommunity is somewhat less likely in our individualistic society, but some couples do focus so much on building and maintaining their marriages that they neglect to nurture themselves as individuals. For example, if Keri, the woman who was unjustly criticized by her husband, had devoted herself solely to taking care of her relationship with her husband, Dan, then their marriage would have remained stunted or ended in divorce. Not only did her attention to her individual well-being help her become a stronger and more confident person, her courage also made it possible for her marriage to become significantly more vibrant.

I believe that we can achieve an ongoing fairness in our marriages by developing a balance between equality with our spouses (with an understanding of how our partners are different from us, and of what is good for each spouse individually) and what is good for our marriages as a whole. It may sound complicated, but most couples do manage to maintain something like this kind of balance in their marriages. Like other virtues, the virtue of justice can be acquired. In the many situations you encounter, the ability to see what is important to you, to your partner, and to your relationship requires judgment or practical wisdom. It is partly a matter of paying attention to what feels right, partly a matter of discussion and negotiation between you and your spouse, and partly a matter of learning from others what justice in marriage means.

Justice is found most clearly where both partners actively participate in pursuing shared goals. Fairness may be apparent only over time, for any given interchange or decision may favor one partner over the other. In a strong marriage, the spouses have shared aims, and they come to trust that each is doing his or her part to make the marriage the kind of relationship they want. Spouses demonstrate their trustworthiness by contributing to the common good in the marriage and by consistently taking their partners' interests into account.

10

How Can All of Us Work Together to Cultivate Strong Marriages?

Pro-marriage policies for the 1990s must strive for a synthesis of the good that we have gained and lost in the past forty years, not for a simple restoration of any previous era.

William A. Galston[1]

Marriage is much more than a relationship between two people. The strongest marriages are partnerships devoted to pursuing worthwhile aims that enhance a couple's relationship, but these shared projects also take the partners beyond themselves as a couple. Yet the authors of most professional and popular books portray strong marriages as a matter of the spouses' feelings toward each other, which are dependent on their communication skills. With some notable exceptions,[2] very few authors recognize that every marriage is profoundly shaped by a vast array of people and by powerful cultural traditions.

We have seen that the myth of marital happiness is a unique if problematic cultural achievement that has grown out of centuries of cultural evolution. We are taught, through an untold number of messages from myriad sources, to desire a mutually satisfying, intimate relationship with a person we choose to marry for love. We hear it so much and so consistently that we take it for granted as the only reasonable option. Such is the power of culture.

If we are to change our approach to marriage, as I think we must, it will require not only individual change or changes in couples but also cultural change. If we want to cultivate stronger marriages, we must, as a culture, reinterpret marriage. The reinterpretation I have offered here—of marriage as a process of building a shared life around life projects—can help guide that change. It can help because it highlights the strengths that already exist in many marriages. Many couples already have marriages that are built on shared purposes and maintained through such virtues as friendship, loyalty, generosity, and justice.

I have tried to provide a framework to understand these strengths and a vocabulary to describe them so that it will be easier to recognize and cultivate this kind of relationship. The absence of a vocabulary that helps us understand and discuss shared, life-defining projects impoverishes our concept of marriage. This lack leaves us with the thin and inconstant terminology of emotion unsupported by more enduring commitments. The lack of an alternative framework forces us to distort our perceptions of our marriages and to narrow our evaluation of our relationships to emotional factors. Our feelings are important, but they are defined, shaped, and channeled through the ongoing goals and activities that make up our lives.

How do we go about changing a culture? It seems like such an enormous undertaking that it is almost absurd to propose it. Yet the truth is that cultures and their traditions are always changing. It is only a question of the direction of change. In the overview of the history of marriage (see Chapter Three), we saw that the Christian religion reshaped marriage in the Middle Ages, the Enlightenment philosophers helped change its course through their encouragement of individualism in the seventeenth and eighteenth centuries, the romantic storytellers of the eighteenth and nineteenth centuries helped create the emotion-focused marriage, and therapists and social scientists have made contemporary marriage therapeutic. These changes have been adopted in their turn because they were articulated persuasively and because they seemed to represent important improvements in marriage or to solve problems that threatened marriage in some way.

In the extraordinarily high rate of divorce and the gradual replacement of marriage with cohabitation, we are seeing an unprecedented decline in the institution of marriage.[3] The prevalence of divorce is due to the discrepancy between our expectations for emotional benefits and what ordinary marriages can actually deliver. Cohabitation is, for the majority of people, a testing ground for marriage, in which two people can decide whether they are compatible enough for marriage before they make a commitment. In other words, the high rate of cohabitation is an important sign of how much fear and ambivalence people have about committing themselves to marriage.

I realize that this book alone will not bring about the kind of massive change we need. Mine is but one voice among millions, but I am far from alone in recognizing the problem. There is a growing movement toward significant change in how we understand marriage and toward taking steps to support and strengthen marriage. Action, some of it on a large scale, is already under way with respect to many of the suggestions I will discuss in this chapter.[4] This book is just one of many aimed at reinterpreting marriage. Yet many of these worthy efforts remain significantly entangled with the myth of marital happiness. For example, one of the most common recommendations for strengthening marriage involves some form of communication skills. And we have seen that communication skills by themselves are indeed a therapeutic method of improving marital happiness. As long as our focus remains on individual satisfaction, we remain squarely within the confines of the myth that has destabilized marriage so much, even if we do manage to improve spouses' communication and satisfaction. If communication skills trainers help couples cultivate partnership marriages, they will foster more enduring bonds than a purely technique-oriented approach can.

Avenues for Strengthening Marriages

Changing our cultural approach to marriage will involve changes in many of our social practices on the part of people in a wide variety of roles. In the following sections, I suggest changes that might be instituted by individuals and families, therapists, churches and synagogues, social scientists, the media, and government to help strengthen marriage.

Individuals and Families

Most of this book has addressed the aims and actions that individuals can adopt to strengthen their marriages. Foremost among my suggestions has been a focus on partnership and the cultivation of the virtues that can help us build flourishing marriages. We can do a great deal as individuals to foster our virtuous inclinations and actions, but none of us can become virtuous all by ourselves. All of us need teachers and heroes in order to become virtuous people.

Families are one of the key arenas in which people can learn virtue. Being a spouse and a partner offers unparalleled opportunities to cultivate and practice virtue. Teaching children to act virtuously is indispensable to their future success, to the strength of their marriages, and to the future of our nation. Aristotle was correct, I think, in recognizing that virtue begins with learning to do the right thing without necessarily knowing all the reasons that make it right. As good habits are being adopted, children can be taught why they should act in particular ways. After this training, they gradually learn to understand and recognize what is at stake in different situations and how best to respond to the multiple demands of any set of circumstances. Virtue education is a long process, but helping our children to become the best people they can be is well worth the effort.

I have also stressed that the most important goods in marriage (and in communities) are those that are held in common. Shared goals define us, our marriages, and our other social attachments.

They give our lives a definitive shape and direction. The majority of our most treasured projects—for example, those involving democracy, justice, solidarity, and the maintenance of valued traditions—can be conducted only in common with others. We are always intricately tied to the people with whom we live, however much we insist that we are independent individuals. Everyone in a community benefits from others' contributions to the community, and everyone owes his or her support to the projects that the community undertakes for the benefit of all. Marriage is a minicommunity in which spouses depend on each other. By recognizing the importance of shared goals, we can see that there is much more that binds a husband and wife together than how much they please each other.

One of the most important things spouses can do to maintain a strong bond with each other is to focus their attention on what unites them rather than on what separates them. In most marriages, the partners are united about the really important things, even if they disagree and argue about many of the details in life. There are, of course, marriages that are hopelessly conflicted, and no amount of attention to the spouses' shared life can overcome that estrangement. When a marriage reaches this point, a divorce may be the best choice. But serious disaffection seldom occurs suddenly. It is far more common for spouses to gradually grow apart, and for differences and wounds to fester over time, until the final result is irremediable breakdown. Because we are all human, all of us will experience hurts, disappointments, and disagreements in our marriages. Our marriages can be maintained by our practice of the virtues of self-restraint, courage, loyalty, generosity, and justice. Ongoing efforts to heal the inevitable breaches and difficulties in our relationships are needed to maintain the character friendship that makes for a vibrant partnership marriage.

If having a partnership is an important part of building a lifelong marriage, then deciding whom to marry is absolutely critical. There is a cultural message, continuously blaring at us from all sides, that romantic love is the only acceptable motive for marriage. Romantic attraction is a beautiful thing, but it is simply not enough. Real love is more than just a feeling. It is a commitment to someone and to the life that you share. This kind of love develops over time as you participate in joint projects with your spouse. Real love can develop only if two people can become partners in at least some of their life projects. Choosing a mate requires more than paying attention to sexual and emotional attraction. We must use our minds and our judgment, as well as our hearts, to pick a spouse with whom we can share the most important projects and goals of our lives.

Therapists

A number of recent books—William Doherty's *Soul Searching*, Philip Cushman's *Constructing the Self, Constructing America,* and *Re-envisioning Psychology,* which I coauthored with Frank Richardson and Charles Guignon—show that therapy is an unavoidably moral endeavor.[5] Doherty's book is interesting because he presents the moral dimension of therapy primarily in terms of virtue. Doherty actually argues that it is wrong for therapists to try to be neutral in some situations. He describes the importance of many virtues in therapeutic practice, but he stops short of tying these virtues to an understanding of the good life, as Aristotle does.

The idea that good marriages can be developed and maintained through the application of communication techniques is insufficient because, as we have seen, individuals cannot use communication skills well unless they can also exercise self-restraint, courage, and generosity, among other traits. Therefore, any hope we have of strengthening marriages must include a focus on fostering virtue. Because the use of communication skills does require the exercise of virtue, it is clear that therapists cannot avoid the moral dimension of marriage by focusing on communication skills.

Many marital therapists may be uncomfortable with the frankly moral vocabulary of this book. The therapeutic community has always tried to keep moral questions at arm's length by maintaining an apparently neutral position with regard to moral matters. The various professions have codes of ethical behavior, but these codes offer only very general guidelines for avoiding harm to clients by maintaining confidentiality, respecting clients' personal values, and so forth. These codes do not offer explicit statements about how therapists should approach a broader range of moral questions, such as the place of virtue in therapy or what makes a marriage good. Professional ethical codes are not the place for setting out what is best in marriage, but this does not mean that therapists can ignore questions of virtues and value. In the end, each therapist and couple must use the best possible judgment to decide what is good in marriage.

Therapists have tried to manage difficult moral questions by attempting to remain neutral and assuming that their clients will make their own moral judgments. This well-intentioned effort to be neutral about values cannot possibly succeed, however, because no one can be truly neutral. Therapists, as human beings, inevitably take stands on what is best in life. Ironically, the belief that everyone is entitled to decide individually which values to adopt is itself a powerful moral commitment: an endorsement of the value of individual self-determination that is at the heart of individualism. Similarly, the prominent therapeutic ideals of individual happiness and satisfaction with marriage are individualistic values.

Marital therapists have not been neutral about the kinds of marriages they promote, either, because they have generally accepted the idea that mutual satisfaction defines a good marriage. Therapists also tend to define marriage therapeutically, seeing spouses as quasi-therapists to each other. These quasi-therapeutic functions of spouses are intended to help each spouse express his or her individuality and overcome childhood hurts.

It is not surprising that therapists should promote these values in their work with couples, for these values fit very neatly into our individualistic culture and into the therapeutic perspective. Yet when therapists promote the pursuit of individual happiness and the exercise of mutual therapeutic grooming as ways to have a good marriage, they forfeit their neutrality. The only surprising thing is that therapists ever thought they could be neutral about what is valuable and important in marriage in the context of helping couples create better relationships.

If therapists are going to take some stand on what is good in marriage, I believe that the partnership marriage I have described in this book provides a very appealing alternative to an exclusive focus on marriage as a source of individual gratification. When therapists discuss a couple's goals for therapy, they can focus on highlighting the shared projects that unite a couple and that can significantly enhance the reinvigoration of the spouses' attachment to each other. By exploring the life projects that the partners share, therapists can help spouses renew their commitment to each other and their sense of common purpose.

When therapists teach communication skills, they need to recognize that such virtues as self-restraint, courage, and generosity are necessary to the use of these skills. In some cases, the spouses may need to develop their capacity to enact these virtues before they can use communication skills. In other instances, therapists may need only to remind and encourage the partners to enact these traits in communicating with each other.

Therapists can also enhance their effectiveness by fostering the practice of the other virtues we have explored in this book. They help foster bonds of friendship between the partners, bonds forged through mutual enjoyment, shared suffering, and mutual involvement in the everyday tasks and activities of ordinary life. Therapists can also recognize and encourage the loyalty that partners have for each other. They can encourage partners to practice generosity and thus help them recapture their ability to see the best in each other and forgive the wounds they have inflicted on each other. They can help couples cultivate trustworthiness in their marriages by fostering the virtue of justice in the marriage, balancing the needs of the two individuals with those of the couple and dealing constructively with differences between the spouses.

Churches and Synagogues

Mike and Harriet McManus, the founders of Marriage Savers, have taken the clergy to task for allowing pro-marriage traditions to weaken.[6] They note that about three-quarters of first marriages are celebrated in churches and synagogues. This means that clergy have access to most couples. But clergy, the McManuses believe, have not made the most of this access to promote strong marriages. The Mc-Manuses suggest that congregations can do much more to prepare couples for lifelong marriage, to strengthen marriages from within churches and synagogues, and to save distressed relationships. They call many churches "blessing machines" or "wedding factories" that grind out weddings every weekend, with no strategy for helping these marriages succeed. Yet they recognize the enormous demands on the clergy, and they recommend that lay couples, organized and encouraged by members of the clergy, do much of this work.

The McManuses believe that churches and synagogues should include the strengthening of marriage as an important part of their ministries. They advocate several steps that religious organizations can take to promote this goal. The first of these is to institute marriage-preparation programs that help engaged couples reflect on their relationships and learn about how to have a good marriage. There are premarital inventories, such as one called PREPARE,[7] that are designed to help couples reflect on the strengths and weaknesses of their relationships.

I have seen the importance of marital preparation firsthand. I have given the premarital inventory PREPARE to dozens of couples and found that a surprising number of couples have very strained relationships before marriage. Most of these couples believe that everything will work out fine, simply because they love each other. Unfortunately, our studies have shown that trouble in the engagement does not disappear. Distressed relationships before marriage very frequently lead to divorce.

The important thing is to help couples improve their relationships before marriage, and to make it clear that there is help available after marriage, or to help couples avoid marriages that appear doomed from the beginning. Of course, the decision about whether to marry is always up to the couple; counselors and clergy should not pressure couples one way or the other. But providing the opportunity for couples to reflect on the strengths and difficulties of their relationships before they marry is an invaluable service.

Several studies suggest that marital preparation can help couples have better marriages.[8] Many marriage-preparation programs focus primarily on improvements in couples' communication and leisure-time activities, as well as on the sexual relationship. I think that these are important parts of marriage and that learning skills in these areas can be helpful. I am also convinced that skills training needs to be supplemented with work aimed at cultivating the virtues necessary for good communication. In addition, it is essential that couples hear from clergy and professionals that a good marriage is more than a happy or satisfying marriage. Engaged couples need to know that marriage, at its best, is a shared life devoted to worthwhile projects that define the relationship and the spouses' lives.

The McManuses also encourage churches and synagogues, as a second step, both to help married couples in strengthening their relationships and to offer assistance to troubled marriages. There are many programs available to accomplish these goals, although I would add the same caveat about them that I did about premarital programs: enhancing marital satisfaction through training in communication skills is good, but it is not enough.

Many pastors, priests, and rabbis do not have the time to conduct these programs on their own. They do not need to, however, because volunteer couples can be trained to conduct marital programs. These couples can mentor other couples as they learn about marriage and about the skills and virtues that lead to a strong marriage. An extensive listing of these programs is available from the Coalition for Marriage, Family, and Couples Education.[9]

The most far-reaching suggestion the McManuses have made is for the creation of Community Marriage Policies, whereby civic leaders and clergy from many denominations would unite in promoting stronger marriages in their communities as a whole. These policies would involve minimum standards for marital preparation, in addition to agreements to set up programs for strengthening existing marriages. This community-based approach offers clergy local support and encouragement for including marriage in their ministries. Perhaps more important, this approach sets the tone for an entire community about the importance and worthiness of strong marriages, and it helps establish the idea of marriage as a lifelong commitment to something more than personal happiness.

Social Scientists

The first thing social scientists can do to help improve marriages is to recognize that up to now they have been guided by an individualistic understanding of marriage, one that has highlighted personal satisfaction as defining a good marriage. In their theories and investigations, social scientists have adopted the premises of the myth of marital happiness. They need to question this myth and look beyond it for a better understanding of what makes strong marriages possible. Once researchers understand that they have limited their investigations to only one of many possible elements of what is good in marriage, they can help shed additional light on other ways to understand marriage. For example, investigation into partnership marriages can help us better understand how some spouses forge strong bonds with each other and maintain their ability to cooperate in their shared life through thick and thin.

It is time that social scientists recognized that they have promoted an individualistic ideal of marriage and that the value-neutrality they seek has eluded them. This recognition can help researchers broaden their focus to include things that tie partners together more profoundly than can pleasure and constraint. Until now, there has been no place in scientific theories of marriage for partnership or for the virtues that are so deeply implicated in strong marriages. The individualistic perspective of social scientists has made these aspects of marriage all but invisible to them.

The Media

Sex, passion, and romance are powerful themes in entertainment, and they are relatively easy to portray. A love interest is a staple in movies, television, and books, and most of the time the romance unfolds in an unmarried couple. All too often, the story ends when the couple falls in love and starts life together. This is an unabashed endorsement of the myth of marital happiness because the story conveys that falling in love is a more important part of marriage than building a shared life. This kind of story tells us that everything will simply fall into place because people love each other.

We need to see more portrayals of couples who work together to accomplish their life projects and make their lives meaningful. There is great drama and humor in the everyday struggles of married life, and there have been memorable (and very popular) depictions of the ways in which couples maintain their bonds to each other through challenges and difficulties. Increasing the proportion of stories that focus on the development of a strong marriage can help greatly in providing encouragement and guidance to married people. We need stories that inspire us to be better spouses and that call on spouses to pursue worthwhile aims together.

Similarly, the news media are far more likely to present us with stories of discord, infidelity, and divorce. Such stories are far more titillating and sensational than stories about the life projects that couples share. Presenting stories about the value and beauty of partnership marriages is more challenging but far more useful to our society. People are fascinated and sometimes amused when celebrities stumble in their marriages, but we also need instructive examples of how couples have managed to build strong marriages against the odds in our individualistic society.

It is a truism that the entertainment industry wields great power in influencing people in this country and in much of the rest of the world. The historic effects of the rise of the romantic novel testify to this power. But this power to influence comes with a responsibility. The more the entertainment media portray love as little more than romantic attraction, and the more they neglect to present us with images of strong, stable marriages, the more people will believe that passion and gratification are the sole indicators of a good relationship. We all need models and examples of people who are able to exemplify lives of purpose and character, and I am challenging the entertainment and news media to provide more of them.

Stories of friendship, loyalty, generosity, and justice in marriage can go a long way toward helping couples recognize and cultivate these virtues. It is important that reporters and writers avoid the easy temptation to portray virtuous action as priggish or hypocritical unless such a depiction is clearly warranted. Our cultural rejection of Victorian morals includes a very heavy dose of derision for those who present themselves publicly as virtuous but pursue their vices privately. There is no doubt that this derision has been deserved, to some degree, but portraying virtue primarily in such negative terms is a grave injustice to those who practice it naturally and without pretense. It is a far too easy, jaundiced way to cater to the lowest part of our nature and avoid the rigors of goodness.

Government

The high rate of divorce and its negative consequences have encouraged many to focus on increasing the legal obstacles to divorce. But divorce is not the problem, as I have said before. It is a symptom, so tightening the divorce laws will accomplish little. The history of divorce law and practice demonstrates clearly that people who want a divorce will find a way to get one unless divorce is prohibited altogether. No-fault divorce laws were enacted partly because divorcing spouses had so thoroughly circumvented the divorce restrictions that existed at that time that it no longer made sense to restrict divorce. It is far better to seek ways of strengthening marriage so that spouses will be less interested in divorce than to try to legislate marital stability.

As noted earlier (see Chapter Seven), Louisiana and Arizona have enacted covenant marriage laws that allow the couple to choose between an ordinary marriage, which can be dissolved by either partner, and a covenant marriage, which involves a higher level of commitment. Many other states are considering similar laws. Allowing couples to choose between an ordinary marriage and a covenant marriage is one of the most attractive features of this law because it avoids the negative effects of governmental coercion. In addition, by making the kind of marriage a choice, these state legislatures have created an important opportunity for the prospective spouses to thoughtfully consider and discuss their degree of commitment to each other and to consider what kind of marriage they hope to have. A covenant marriage restores the idea that marriage is intended to be a lifelong commitment. It is also possible for an already married couple to "upgrade" their marriage to a covenant marriage.

Louisiana's law contains three concrete features that can strengthen marriages: couples who choose covenant marriages also agree to participate in marital preparation of some kind; if serious difficulties arise in the marriage, the partners legally commit themselves to taking all reasonable steps (counseling included) to resolve the difficulties; if a divorce is contested (that is, if one spouse wants to divorce, and the other does not), there is a two-year waiting period for the divorce, which allows time for reconciliation.

Some other states have instituted laws that offer financial incentives for marital preparation. Florida, for example, reduces the fees that a couple pays for a marriage license when the prospective spouses participate in some form of marital preparation. Once again, this law creates an opportunity for choice and discussion as a couple approaches marriage. The availability of covenant marriage and the incentives for marital preparation need to be publicized and promoted by government in order to encourage couples to consciously choose whether to participate in these marriage-strengthening opportunities.

Married couples experience many strains in our society, given the demands of both partners working and caring for their children. These strains can undermine even the strongest marriage. Governments can adopt policies to ease these burdens and thereby support marriage. Creating a more generous family-leave policy is among the top priorities, so that a parent can take time off for child care. Current policy offers a very brief period of unpaid leave, which guarantees benefits and the right to resume employment. These provisions are a step in the right direction, but our investment in marriage and in children needs to be strengthened by the provision of paid leave, with the possibility of its being extending (with or without pay).

Can We Move Beyond the Myth?

There is really little question as to whether we will move beyond the myth of marital happiness. It is unsustainable, and it is already beginning to collapse. The current trend is for fewer people to marry, for half of all marriages to last fewer than seven years, and for the majority of recent marriages to end in divorce. As a result, more and more couples live together without marrying. As long as we try to maintain our unreasonable expectations of marriage as an avenue for personal pleasure, the decline of marriage will continue.

We can change our preoccupation with satisfaction in marriage and focus our attention more on creating strong partnership marriages. By agreeing on shared goals, couples can give their marriages greater purpose and stability. The life projects that define our individual and married lives do not have to be lofty or grandiose, although some will be. Pursuing a good family life, raising responsible and productive children, and continuing family and civic traditions are all worthy of considerable devotion and mutual effort.

When we pursue these kinds of worthwhile aims, we rise above the squalid machinations of the exclusively self-interested and make our shared lives shine with purpose and commitment. Partnership marriages make it possible for couples to contribute to their traditions and their nation in essential and enduring ways. Participating as a couple in voter registration, public arts and crafts shows, scouting, or any number of other worthy projects binds spouses to the purposes and meanings that have guided and enriched the lives of generations of Americans. When we devote ourselves to projects that take us beyond our narrow personal interests, we join the ongoing stream of life. Our lives take on richness, meaning, and dignity that go far beyond what is possible in the pursuit of individual happiness. Marriages in which the partners pursue the good together are immeasurably stronger than those devoted solely to satisfaction.

The cultivation of the virtues described in this book will also strengthen marriages dramatically. Striving to develop and maintain good character makes it possible to pursue the goals that make life worthwhile. Practicing virtue helps to build vibrant marriages and flourishing lives because people of character act virtuously in all arenas of their lives.

Marriage offers one of the best opportunities we have to develop character. Its importance and centrality make it a crucible where our mettle is continually tested and refined. In the everyday experiences and demands of marriage, we have myriad opportunities to cultivate virtue and demonstrate quality of character. There are many similar opportunities in parenting, in our working lives, and in our public lives, but marriage is one of the most intense and enduring settings for us to become the best people we can be.

Individuals, families, therapists, churches and synagogues, the media, and government can all play important roles in fostering virtue, which is very much a concern of the community and of the nation. Without it, marriages will continue to disintegrate, and those who do practice virtue will lack the vocabulary and the encouragement that could support their continued efforts.

The question of our marriages' strength is far too important for us simply accept the status quo. We must make every effort to encourage and support strong marriages for ourselves, for our children, and for our nation. Our inclination to understand marriage as an emotion-based, private affair between two people is one of the great tragedies of our time. The romantic approach to marriage has been, in many ways, a noble and exciting experiment, but we now know that it has failed, and we must find another way to strengthen this vital institution. I hope this book has shed some light on how we can engage in this crucial endeavor.

Chapter Notes

1. The Guidance of Myth

1. Daniel J. Boorstin, *The Image: A Guide to Pseudo-Events in America*. (New York: Atheneum, 1962), p. 6.

2. Tim B. Heaton and Stan L. Albrecht, "Stable Unhappy Marriages," *Journal of Marriage and the Family* 53 (1991), 747–758; Robert Schoen and Robin M. Weinick, "The Slowing Metabolism of Marriages: Figures from 1988 U.S. Marital Status Life Tables," *Demography* 30 (1993), 737–746.

3. Joseph Campbell and Bill Moyers, *The Power of Myth*. (New York: Doubleday, 1988), p. 15.

4. Robert N. Bellah, Richard Madsen, William M. Sullivan, Ann Swidler, and Stephen M. Tipton, *Habits of the Heart: Individualism and Commitment in American Life*. (Berkeley: University of California Press, 1985).

5. Béroul, *The Romance of Tristan*, trans. Alan Fedrick. (New York: Penguin, 1970).

6. Campbell and Moyers, *The Power of Myth*, p. 190.

7. Larry Bumpass, "What's Happening to the Family? Interactions between Demographic and Institutional Change," *Demography* 27 (1990), 483–498; Teresa C. Martin and Larry Bumpass, "Recent Trends in Marital Disruption," *Demography* 26 (1989), 37–52; David Popenoe, "American Family Decline, 1960–1990: A Review and

Appraisal," *Journal of Marriage and the Family* 55 (1993), 527–555; Robert Schoen and Robin M. Weinick, "The Slowing Metabolism of Marriages."

8. Ernest M. Burgess and Leonard S. Cottrell, *Predicting Success or Failure in Marriage*. (New York: Prentice Hall, 1939); Frank D. Fincham and Thomas N. Bradbury, "Perceived Responsibility for Marital Events: Egocentric or Partner-centric Bias?" *Journal of Marriage and the Family*, 51 (1989) 27–35; Frank D. Fincham, Steven R. Beach, and Donald H. Baucom, "Attribution Processes in Distressed and Nondistressed Couples: Self-Partner Attribution Differences." *Journal of Personality and Social Psychology* 52 (1987), 739–748; Blaine J. Fowers, Eileen M. Lyons, Kelly H. Montel, and Netta Shaked, "Positive Illusions About Marriage Among Married and Single Individuals," unpublished manuscript (2000); Lewis M. Terman, *Psychological Factors in Marital Happiness*. (New York: McGraw-Hill, 1938).

2. The Magic Union

1. Robert N. Bellah, Richard Madsen, William M. Sullivan, Ann Swidler, and Stephen M. Tipton, *Habits of the Heart: Individualism and Commitment in American Life*. (Berkeley: University of California Press, 1985), p. 98.

2. Augustus Y. Napier, *The Fragile Bond: In Search of an Equal, Intimate, and Enduring Marriage*. (New York: HarperCollins, 1988), p. 14.

3. Angus Campbell, Paul Converse, and William L. Rodgers, *The Quality of American Life: Perceptions, Evaluations and Satisfactions*. (New York: Russell Sage Foundation, 1976); Norval D. Glenn and Charles N. Weaver, "The Contribution of Marital Happiness to Global Happiness," *Journal of Marriage and the Family* 43 (1981), 161–168.

4. Joseph Veroff, Elizabeth Douvan, and Shirley J. Hatchett, *Marital Instability: A Social and Behavioral Study of the Early Years*. (New York: Praeger, 1995), p. xii.

5. Catherine E. Ross, "The Intersection of Work and Family: The Sense of Personal Control and Well-Being of Women and Men,"

paper presented at Family Structure and Health conference, San Francisco, Aug. 1989.

6. Catherine E. Ross, John Mirowski, and Karen Goldstein, "The Impact of the Family on Health: A Decade in Review," *Journal of Marriage and the Family* 52 (1990), 1059–1078; Lisa Berkman and S. Leonard Syme, "Social Networks, Host Resistance, and Mortality: A Nine-Year Follow-up Study of Alameda County Residents," *American Journal of Epidemiology* 109 (1979), 186-204; Lee Lillard and Linda Waite, "'Til Death Do Us Part': Marital Disruption and Mortality," *American Journal of Sociology* 100 (1995), 1131–1156; Eugene Litwack and Peter Messeri, "Organizational Theory, Social Supports, and Mortality Rates: A Theoretical Convergence," *American Sociological Review* 54 (1989), 49–66. For discussions of the mental health benefits of marriage, see Walter Gove, "The Relationship Between Sex Roles, Mental Illness and Marital Status," *Social Forces* 51 (1973), 34–44; Walter Gove, Michael Hughes, and Carolyn Style, "Does Marriage Have Positive Effects on the Psychological Well-Being of the Individual?" *Journal of Health and Social Behavior* 24 (1983), 122–131; Deborah Williams, "Gender, Marriage and Psychosocial Well-Being," *Journal of Family Issues* 9 (1988), 452–468. A number of studies have documented the fact that being married decreases the risk of suicide and that divorce increases this risk. See Steven Stack, "New Micro-level Data on the Impact of Divorce on Suicide, 1959-1980: A Test of Two Theories," *Journal of Marriage and the Family* 52 (1990), 119–127; David Lester, *Why People Kill Themselves.* (Springfield, Ill.: Charles C. Thomas, 1992); Ronald Maris, *Pathways to Suicide.* (Baltimore: Johns Hopkins University Press, 1981); Ira Wasserman, "The Impact of Divorce on Suicide in the U.S.," *Family Perspective* 24 (1990), 61–68.

7. Jessie Bernard, *The Future of Marriage.* (New York: Bantam Books, 1972).

8. Julia S. Brown and Barbara Giesy, "Marital Status of Persons with Spinal Cord Injury," *Social Science and Medicine* 23 (1986), 313–322.

9. For discussions of marriage as the most important source of social support, see Michael Argyle and Adrian Furnham, "Sources of

Satisfaction and Conflict in Long-Term Relationships," *Journal of Marriage and the Family* 45 (1983), 481-493; Sheldon Cohen and S. Leonard Syme, "Issues in the Study and Application of Social Support," in Sheldon Cohen and S. Leonard Syme (eds.), *Social Support and Health*. (Orlando, Fla.: Academic Press, 1985), pp. 3–23; Kenneth Heller, Ralph Swindle, and Linda Dusenbury, "Component Social Support Processes: Comments and Integration," *Journal of Consulting and Clinical Psychology* 54 (1986), 466–470; Danny Hoyt and Nicholas Babchuk, "Adult Kinship Networks: The Selective Formation of Intimate Ties with Kin," *Social Forces* 62 (1983), 84–101; Lawrence Kurdek, "Social Support and Psychological Distress in First-Married and Remarried Newlywed Husbands and Wives," *Journal of Marriage and the Family* 51 (1989), 1047–1052; Morton Lieberman, "Social Supports—The Consequences of Psychologizing: A Commentary," *Journal of Consulting and Clinical Psychology* 54 (1986), 461–465. Other authors describe the frequency with which spouses are cited as primary confidants. In this connection, see Bradford Brown, "Social and Psychological Correlates of Help-Seeking Behavior Among Urban Adults," *American Journal of Community Psychology* 6 (1978), 425–439; Danny Hoyt and Nicholas Babchuk, "Adult Kinship Networks."

10. See Arland Thornton, "Changing Attitudes Toward Family Issues in the United States," *Journal of Marriage and the Family* 51 (1989), 873–893; Arland Thornton and David Freedman, "Changing Attitudes Toward Marriage and Single Life," *Family Planning Perspectives* 14 (1982), 297–303; Robert Schoen, William Urton, Karen Woodrow, and John Baj, "Marriage and Divorce in Twentieth-Century American Cohorts," *Demography* 22 (1985), 101–114; Paul C. Glick, "Fifty Years of Family Demography: A Record of Social Change," *Journal of Marriage and the Family* 50 (1988), 861–873.

11. Robert Schoen and Robin M. Weinick, "The Slowing Metabolism of Marriages: Figures from 1988 U.S. Marital Status Life Tables," *Demography* 30 (1993), 737–746; Larry L. Bumpass, James A. Sweet, and Andrew Cherlin, "The Role of Cohabitation in Declining Rates of Marriage," *Journal of Marriage and the Family* 53 (1991), 913–927; Larry L. Bumpass and James A. Sweet, "National Esti-

mates of Cohabitation: Cohort Levels and Union Stability," *Demography* 26 (1989), 615–625.

12. Bumpass, Sweet, and Cherlin, "The Role of Cohabitation in Declining Rates of Marriage"; Neil G. Bennett, Ann K. Blanc, and David E. Bloom, "Commitment and the Modern Union: Assessing the Link between Premarital Cohabitation and Subsequent Marital Stability, *American Sociological Review* 53 (1988), 127–138; Bumpass and Sweet, "National Estimates of Cohabitation"; Jay D. Teachman and Karen A. Polonko, "Cohabitation and Marital Stability in the United States," *Social Forces* 69 (1990), 207-220; Elizabeth Thomson and Ugo Colella, "Cohabitation and Marital Stability: Quality or Commitment?" *Journal of Marriage and the Family* 54 (1992), 259–267.

13. Catherine Reissman, *Divorce Talk: Women and Men Make Sense of Personal Relationships*. (New Brunswick, N.J.: Rutgers University Press, 1990), pp. 23–24, 72.

14. Andrew Cherlin, *Marriage, Divorce, and Remarriage*. (Cambridge, Mass.: Harvard University Press, 1992); Paul Glick, "Marriage, Divorce, and Living Arrangements: Prospective Changes," *Journal of Family Issues* 5 (1984), 6–26; United Nations Department of International Economic and Social Affairs Statistical Office, *Demographic Yearbook, 1983*. (New York: United Nations Department of International Economic and Social Affairs Statistical Office, 1985).

15. Cherlin, *Marriage, Divorce, and Remarriage*; James A. Sweet and Larry L. Bumpass, *American Families and Households*. (New York: Russell Sage Foundation, 1987); Lynn White and Alan Booth, "The Quality and Stability of Remarriages: The Role of Stepchildren," *American Sociological Review* 50 (1985), 689–698.

16. Rachel R. Barich and Denise D. Bielby, "Rethinking Marriage: Change and Stability in Expectations, 1967–1994," *Journal of Family Issues* 17 (1996), 162.

17. Judith Wallerstein and Sandra Blakeslee, *The Good Marriage*. (Boston: Houghton Mifflin, 1995), p. 5.

18. Robert N. Bellah, Richard Madsen, William M. Sullivan, Ann Swidler, and Stephen M. Tipton, *Habits of the Heart: Individualism and*

Commitment in American Life. Berkeley, Calif.: University of California Press, 1985), p. 91.

19. Wallerstein and Blakeslee, *The Good Marriage*, p. 239.

20. Blaine J. Fowers and David H. Olson, "ENRICH Marital Satisfaction Scale: A Reliability and Validity Study," *Journal of Family Psychology* 7 (1993), 1–10; David H. Olson, David G. Fournier, and Joan M. Druckman, *Counselor's Manual for PREPARE/ENRICH* (Minneapolis: PREPARE/ENRICH, 1987); Douglas K. Snyder, *Marital Satisfaction Inventory Manual*. (Los Angeles: Western Psychological Services, 1981).

21. Howard Markman, Scott Stanley, and Susan L. Blumberg, *Fighting for Your Marriage*. (San Francisco: Jossey-Bass, 1994), p. 84.

22. Bellah, Madsen, Sullivan, Swidler, and Tipton, *Habits of the Heart*, p. 93.

3. How Did We Get Here?

1. George Eliot, *Middlemarch: A Study of Provincial Life*. (New York: MacMillan, 1926), p. 821.

2. Lambert, *History of the Counts of Guines*, cited in George Duby, *Medieval Marriage*. (Baltimore: Johns Hopkins University Press, 1978), pp. 88, 91.

3. Eric J. Carlson, *Marriage and the English Reformation*. (Oxford, England: Blackwell, 1994).

4. Lawrence Stone, *The Family, Sex, and Marriage*. (New York: HarperCollins, 1977).

5. Carlson, *Marriage and the English Reformation*.

6. Stone, *The Family, Sex, and Marriage*.

7. Stone, *The Family, Sex, and Marriage*.

8. Stone, *The Family, Sex, and Marriage*.

9. Stone, *The Family, Sex, and Marriage*.

10. Stone, *The Family, Sex, and Marriage*.

11. Roderick Phillips, *Putting Asunder: A History of Divorce in Western Society*. (Cambridge, England: Cambridge University Press, 1988).

12. Stone, *The Family, Sex, and Marriage*.

13. Stone, *The Family, Sex, and Marriage*.

14. Stone, *The Family, Sex, and Marriage*.

15. Stone, *The Family, Sex, and Marriage*.

16. Phillips, *Putting Asunder*; J. Herbie DiFonzo, *Beneath the Fault Line: The Popular and Legal Culture of Divorce in Twentieth-Century America*. (Charlottesville: University Press of Virginia, 1997).

17. Philips, *Putting Asunder*, p. 10.

18. Elaine Tyler May, *Great Expectations: Marriage and Divorce in Post-Victorian America*. (Chicago: University of Chicago Press, 1980), p. 47.

19. May, *Great Expectations*.

20. May, *Great Expectations*.

21. May, *Great Expectations*, p. 90.

22. May, *Great Expectations*, p. 144.

23. DiFonzo, *Beneath the Fault Line*.

24. George A. Bartlett, *Men, Women and Conflict: An Intimate Study of Love, Marriage and Divorce*. (New York: G. P. Putnam, 1939), p. 14.

25. Robert Schoen, William Urton, Karen Woodrow, and John Baj, "Marriage and Divorce in Twentieth-Century American Cohorts," *Demography* 22 (1985), 101–114.

26. Joseph Veroff, Elizabeth Douvan, and Richard A. Kulka, *The Inner American: A Self-Portrait from 1957 to 1976*. (New York: Basic Books, 1981).

27. Barbara Defoe Whitehead, *The Divorce Culture*. (New York: Knopf, 1997).

28. DiFonzo, *Beneath the Fault Line*; Phillips, *Putting Asunder*; Lenore Weitzman, *The Divorce Revolution*. (New York: Free Press, 1985).

29. Phillips, *Putting Asunder*.

30. Weitzman, *The Divorce Revolution*, pp. 367–368.

31. John Gray, *What Your Mother Didn't Tell You and Your Father Didn't Know*. (New York: HarperCollins), pp. 7–8.

32. Stone, *The Family, Sex, and Marriage*, p. 425.

4. Marital Therapy, the Science of Marriage, and the Myth

1. Augustus Y. Napier, *The Fragile Bond: In Search of an Equal, Intimate, and Enduring Marriage*. (New York: HarperCollins, 1988), p. 14.

2. John M. Gottman, James Coan, Sybil Carrere, and Catherine Swanson, "Predicting Marital Happiness and Stability from Newlywed Interactions." *Journal of Marriage and the Family* 60 (1998), 5–22.

3. Harville Hendrix, *Getting the Love You Want: A Guide for Couples*. (New York: Harper, 1966).

4. Marian Sandmaier, "Love for the Long Haul," *Family Therapy Networker*, Sept./Oct. 1997, pp. 26, 28 (emphasis in original).

5. Napier, *The Fragile Bond*, p. 14.

6. Philip Rieff, *The Triumph of the Therapeutic: Uses of Faith After Freud*. (New York: Harper, 1966).

7. John M. Gottman, *What Predicts Divorce: The Relationship between Marital Processes and Marital Outcomes*. (Hillsdale, N.J.: Erlbaum, 1994).

8. Elaine Tyler May, *Great Expectations: Marriage and Divorce in Post-Victorian America*. (Chicago: University of Chicago Press, 1980), p. 63.

5. Creating the Good Marriage

1. Henry David Thoreau, *Essays and Other Writings*, Will H. Durks, ed. (New York: Walter Scott Publishing, 1985), p. 140.

2. Aristotle, *The Works of Aristotle*, trans. W. D. Ross. (London: Humphrey Milford, 1925), 1228a, 1–2.

3. Sarah Broadie, *Ethics with Aristotle*. (New York: Oxford University Press, 1991).

4. It is important to acknowledge and disavow Aristotle's views on the nature of men and women. He saw men as morally superior to

women. From this point of view, then, there will always be inequality in male-female relationships, marriage included. This perspective was an aspect of Aristotle's cultural context, but it is one that we no longer see as accurate or desirable. There is no reason for us to retain the notion of inequality in the moral worth of the sexes, nor does Aristotle's account of the virtues, and particularly of friendship, require this inequality. My discussion of the virtues and of friendship assumes the moral equality of men and women.

5. Aristotle, *Nichomachean Ethics*, trans. Martin Ostwald. (Indianapolis: Bobbs-Merrill, 1962).

6. Aristotle. *Nichomachean Ethics*, p. 50.

7. Alasdair MacIntyre, *After Virtue: A Study in Moral Theory*. (Notre Dame, Ind.: University of Notre Dame Press, 1981).

6. The Virtue of Friendship

1. Aristotle, *Nichomachean Ethics*, trans. Martin Ostwald. (Indianapolis: Bobbs-Merrill, 1962), p. 214.

2. Jimmy Carter, *Why Not the Best?* (Nashville: Broadman Press, 1975), pp. 69–70.

3. Douglas Brinkley, *The Unfinished Presidency*. (New York: Viking, 1998).

7. The Virtue of Loyalty

1. Simone Signoret, *Nostalgia Isn't What It Used to Be*. (New York: Harper & Row, 1978), p. 222.

2. George Fletcher, *Loyalty*. (Oxford: Oxford University Press, 1993), pp. 8–9.

3. Hans Georg Gadamer, *Truth and Method*. (New York: Continuum Publishing Group, 1975), p. 245.

4. Fletcher, *Loyalty*. (Oxford: Oxford University Press, 1993.)

5. Martin Heidegger, *Being and Time*, trans. J. Macquarrie and E. Robinson. (New York: HarperCollins, 1962). I am particularly

indebted to my good friend Charles Guignon for my understanding of Heidegger's stimulating but very challenging work.

6. Gay C. Kitson, *Portrait of Divorce: Adjustment to Marital Breakdown*. (New York: Guilford Press, 1992); Catherine Reissman, *Divorce Talk: Women and Men Make Sense of Personal Relationships*. (New Brunswick, N.J.: Rutgers University Press, 1990); Diane Vaughan, *Uncoupling: Turning Points in Intimate Relationships*. (Oxford: Oxford University Press, 1986).

8. The Virtue of Generosity

1. Percy Bysshe Shelley, *Prometheus Unbound: A Lyrical Drama*. (Boston: D. C. Heath, 1892), p. 112.

9. The Virtue of Justice

1. Charles Taylor, "Justice After Virtue," in *After MacIntyre*, John Horton and Susan Mendus, eds. (Notre Dame, Ind.: Notre Dame University Press), p. 37.

2. Ivan Boszormenyi-Nagy and Barbara R. Krasner, *Between Give and Take*. (New York: Brunner/Mazel, 1986).

3. Larry L. Bumpass, "What's Happening to the Family? Interactions between Demographic and Institutional Change," *Demography* 27, 1990, 483–498.

4. Aristotle, *Nichomachean Ethics*, trans. Martin Ostwald. (Indianapolis: Bobbs-Merrill, 1962).

5. Robert N. Bellah, Richard Madsen, William M. Sullivan, Ann Swidler, and Stephen M. Tipton, *Habits of the Heart: Individualism and Commitment in American Life*. (Berkeley: University of California Press, 1985); Robert N. Bellah, Richard Madsen, William M. Sullivan, Ann Swidler, and Stephen M. Tipton, *The Good Society*. (New York: Knopf, 1991); Amatai Etzioni, *The Spirit of Community: Rights, Responsibilities, and the Communitarian Agenda*. (New York: Crown, 1993). See also *The Responsive Community*, the journal published by the Communitarian Network.

10. How Can All of Us Work Together to Cultivate Strong Marriages?

1. William A. Galston, "The Reinstitutionalization of Marriage: Political Theory and Public Policy," in *Promises to Keep: Decline and Renewal of Marriage in America*, David Popenoe, Jean Bethke Elshtain, and David Blankenhorn, eds. (Lanham, Md.: Rowman and Littlefield), p. 283.

2. Robert N. Bellah, Richard Madsen, William M. Sullivan, Ann Swidler, and Stephen M. Tipton, *Habits of the Heart: Individualism and Commitment in American Life*. (Berkeley: University of California Press, 1985); Maggie Gallagher, *The Abolition of Marriage*. (Washington, D.C.: Regnery, 1996); David Popenoe, Jean Bethke Elshtain, and David Blankenhorn (eds.), *Promises to Keep*.

3. David Popenoe, "American Family Decline, 1960–1990: A Review and Appraisal," *Journal of Marriage and the Family* 55 (1993), 527–555.

4. David Popenoe, *Life Without Father*. (New York: Free Press, 1996); Popenoe, Elshtain, and Blankenhorn, *Promises to Keep*.

5. Philip Cushman, *Constructing the Self, Constructing America: A Cultural History of Psychotherapy*. (Reading, Mass.: Addison-Wesley, 1995); William J. Doherty, *Soul Searching: Why Psychotherapy Must Promote Moral Responsibility*. (New York: Basic Books, 1995); Frank C. Richardson, Blaine J. Fowers, and Charles Guignon, *Re-envisioning Psychology: Moral Dimensions of Theory and Practice*. (San Francisco: Jossey-Bass, 1999).

6. Michael J. McManus, *Marriage Savers: Helping Your Friends and Family Stay Married*. (New York: Zondervan, 1995).

7. I have given the premarital inventory PREPARE to dozens of couples and found that all too many have very strained relationships before marriage. Most of these prospective spouses believe that everything will work out simply because they love each other, but when trouble appears during engagement, it does not disappear. A distressed relationship before marriage very frequently ends in divorce. In one of our studies, we found that 10 percent of couples

who took the PREPARE inventory postponed or cancelled their wedding plans; I believe that these couples recognized that their relationships were not strong enough to support marriage. See Blaine J. Fowers and David H. Olson, "Predicting Marital Success with PREPARE: A Predictive Validity Study," *Journal of Marital and Family Therapy* 12 (1986), 403–413; Blaine J. Fowers, Kelly H. Montel, and David H. Olson, "An Examination of the Predictive Validity of an Empirically Based Typology of Engaged Couples," *Journal of Marital and Family Therapy* 22 (1996), 102–119. See also Andrea S. Larsen and David H. Olson, "Predicting Marital Satisfaction Using PREPARE: A Replication Study," *Journal of Marital and Family Therapy* 15 (1989), 311–322. For more information on the PREPARE inventory, call Lifestyle Innovations, Inc., at 1-800-331-1661.

8. See, for example, Howard J. Markman, "The Application of a Behavior Model of Marriage in Predicting Relationship Satisfaction for Couples Planning Marriage," *Journal of Consulting and Clinical Psychology* 47 (1979), 743-749; Howard J. Markman, M. J. Resnick, F. J. Floyd, Scott M. Stanley, and M. Clements, "Preventing Marital Distress Through Communication and Conflict Management Training: A Four- and Five-Year Follow-Up," *Journal of Consulting and Clinical Psychology* 61 (1993), 70-77.

9. An extensive list of these programs is available from the Coalition for Marriage, Family, and Couples Education. For more information, write to the director, Diane Sollee, at 5310 Belt Road NW, Washington, D.C. 20015-3332, or set your browser to www.smartmarriages. com.

About the Author

Blaine J. Fowers is associate professor of counseling psychology at the University of Miami. He has published numerous scientific articles on predicting marital success, identifying different types of marriages, and exploring positive illusions about marriage, and is the coauthor of *Re-envisioning Psychology*. A clinical member of the American Association for Marital and Family Therapy, he is an approved supervisor and a licensed psychologist. Fowers received his Ph.D. degree from the University of Texas at Austin in 1987. He has a fifteen-year marriage with Susan Green and they have two children.

 Index